Behind the Scenes

Behind
the
Scenes

In Which
the Author
Talks About
Ronald and
Nancy Reagan
. . . and Himself

**Michael
K. Deaver
with
Mickey
Herskowitz**

WILLIAM MORROW
and COMPANY, INC.
NEW YORK

Library of Congress Cataloging-in-Publication Data

Deaver, Michael K.
  Behind the scenes.
  Includes index.
  1. Reagan, Ronald. 2. Reagan, Nancy, 1923–
3. Deaver, Michael K.—Friends and associates.
4. United States—Politics and government—1981–
I. Herskowitz, Mickey. II. Title.
E877.D43   1988   973.927′092′2   87-28102
ISBN 0-688-06404-3

Printed in the United States of America

First Edition

1 2 3 4 5 6 7 8 9 10

BOOK DESIGN BY PANDORA SPELIOS

To Carolyn , Amanda, and Blair—to my First Family always.

Acknowledgments

When Laurence Barrett, of *The Washington Post,* called my office at the White House, he had a distinctive way of asking for an anecdote, or a touch of color for a story he was doing.

"How about a few raisins for the pudding?" he would say.

I thank Larry for the thought. I tried to keep it in mind, especially in the passages between chapters. Books need texture, too.

The author owes a special debt to: Barbara Walters, for persuading me that I could write about my friendship with the Reagans, without compromising their trust; to my brother, Bill, for the material and opinions he provided; to my secretary, Janet Harvey, who helped keep the process moving; and to an understanding editor, Lisa Drew, for her support.

Contents

Prologue:
The Cowboy
in the
White House

When the idea for this book was first raised, in early 1986, there was a good deal of admiring talk across the country about the Reagan Luck and the Reagan Touch; his unwavering high rating in the polls; and his ability to delegate authority to the able people he had selected to serve him.

I was one of them.

Less than twelve months later, much of the praise had been replaced with criticism of his hands-off management style. His ratings had taken a pounding from the Iran-Contra scandal, and seven special prosecutors had investigated, were about to begin, or were in the middle of cases that involved members of his administration.

And I was one of them.

As it had been conceived, the book was to be an intimate account of my relationship with Ronald and Nancy Reagan, covering twenty years. It began, as books sometimes do, with an offhand remark at a Washington cocktail party. I had told some inside-the-White-House stories, and Barbara Walters piped up: "You ought to put those into a book."

What I wanted to say has not greatly changed from what I had in mind at the start. But I know some of those thoughts and

11

descriptions will not be taken in quite the same way, not now. The words will be read through a different glass. So be it.

The record of the Reagan presidency, its legacy, its achievements and failures, I gladly leave to the historians. My goal was to reveal Ronald Reagan as I knew him: the most human of American presidents. I set for myself a slightly more difficult task in writing about Nancy: to debunk the myths about the iron matron, in the designer gown, who orchestrated her husband's political career.

If the book is weighted in favor of the Reagans, then this is how I saw them, how I have known them. Others may find some of my insights less than flattering, to them or to me. I have not tried to tailor them to the problems that suddenly swallowed us all.

There was no deliberate effort made here to justify the Reagan policies. He is fully capable of defending them, if any defense is needed. I am not comfortable making moral judgments. Understandably, any such attempt now will be read against the backdrop of my indictment on perjury charges that grew out of congressional hearings into my activities after I left the White House.

I deal with this episode later in the book, and I deny those charges with all my heart and conscience. You probably expected I would.

My problems grew out of the Potomac mentality. There is a certain symbolism here, as there has been through much of the Reagan years.

Westerners have a saying about friends they can trust: "He will do to ride the river with." This was a fairly strong vote of confidence in the days when two men in a canoe had to avoid jagged rocks, waterfalls, and hostile Indians firing from the shore. Sometimes one would go over the side to assure the safety of the other.

Reagan has been pictured more than once as a cowboy in the White House. This was a reference to his affection for that life, as well as his willingness to allow members of his Cabinet, and staff, to take their own chances. Thus a marine colonel named Oliver North became the Cowboy's cowboy. The damage from Iranscam may be years in the measuring.

That much and more was uncertain as the final pages of this book were going to print. But Ronald Reagan remained true to form. There were signs that he might indeed be riding out the storm. He would have done so, as he often has, by turning his humor against himself.

Four months after news of the arms sale to Iran broke, he was a guest at the annual Gridiron Club show in Washington. To an audience composed of the city's most important writers, he said:

"Do you remember the flap when I said the bombing would begin in five minutes? Remember when I fell asleep during my audience with the pope? Remember Bitburg?"

Pause.

"Boy. Those were the good ole days."

He added that he understood that monies missing from a Swiss bank account had gone to the SMU football team. In an oblique reference to the charge that his style was too "detached," he said:

"It's true hard work never killed anybody, but I figure, why take a chance?"

Of course, jokes are not answers. But Reagan was not simply yielding to the trouper within him. He understands the uses of humor. By making jokes at his expense, he was acknowledging that many people no longer see him in the same way, with the same trust or respect. His presidency had been flawed.

Yet the strict political rules, when applied to Ronald Reagan, still would not compute. Polls in May 1987 showed that 62 percent of the American people thought he had lied about not knowing of the diversion of funds from the Iranian arms sale to the Contras in Nicaragua. Yet those who approved of the job he was doing still numbered in the 40s, not much under 50 percent.

There was a funny but poignant moment when Reagan welcomed the members of the Super Bowl champion New York Giants to the White House. In a slip of the tongue, he ended a sentence by referring to "our fans." Then he corrected himself, with a wistful smile: "Your fans, I should say. I don't have many fans anymore."

This book is partly an attempt to find the man behind the smile and the quip, and to define Ronald and Nancy Reagan as fully dimensional people. At bottom, it is a book about friendships in high places, and what happens to them when they go through the compactor of American politics.

1
The Man in
the Emergency
Room

The memories of March 30, 1981, are still the hardest of my life to think or talk about and, I suspect, always will be. Five of us walked out of the Washington Hilton Hotel together, and four were shot. I was the only one not wounded.

Men who return unscathed from combat, I am told, often carry with them feelings of guilt for having been spared while friends and comrades fell. This experience was mine as well.

We know it now as the day the president was shot. That he lived, that he came back stronger than ever, makes it possible to look back with relief at the larger drama. There were even moments of wit and humor, most of them provided by Ronald Reagan.

In every respect the day had been routine. The president had entered the Oval Office at his usual time, 8:45 A.M., to meet with his staff for the first briefing. His calendar had been arranged, months in advance, around a speech he was to make to thirty-five hundred AFL-CIO union members convening at the Hilton. Two appointments, scheduled for later that afternoon, would go unkept.

At 1:30 P.M., Raymond Donovan, the secretary of labor, appeared at the White House to accompany Reagan to the convention. We traveled, as we unavoidably did, in a caravan of five or six limousines. The president's car pulled up and was parked at the curb, twenty-five feet from the hotel's VIP entrance, in order to avoid tying up the circular driveway in front.

There were fifteen cars in the motorcade, a normal number for an appearance within the city. On this day I rode in the control car, third in line, the presidential limo being first. The Secret Service manned the second, or follow-up car, code-named "Halfback." These three cars were known, in security terms, as the "Package," and were not to be separated. On foreign trips, I wound up in heated squabbles over whose vehicle went where. We could not run the risk that some diplomat or general—theirs or ours—might block the control car if the Secret Service suddenly peeled off. The Package stayed intact.

The control car always includes a military aide who carries the so-called Black Box, containing the codes that would enable the president to activate a nuclear response. The box, actually a briefcase of standard size, was known among the Reagan staff as "the football," an oblique reminder of the need not to drop it. The military aides, one from each branch of the service, working in shifts, keep the box within reach of the president twenty-four hours a day. They are an elite group.

Also in the control car were the White House physician, and the senior staff person, who would be responsible for making a decision at the civilian level, given the incapacity of the president.

Reagan's speech was short, general, not meant to make news. I checked my watch. We were on our way out at 2:25 P.M., less than an hour after we had left the White House. I had seen the reporters lined up behind a red velvet rope when we arrived. Now, as we made our exit, I instinctively grabbed Jim Brady, the press secretary, and nudged him through the door first to field their questions. I went next, turning left toward the staff car, with two security men and the president behind me.

I walked around Jim on my way to the other side of the car. I had reached the right rear fender when a reporter called out to the president. He did exactly what I had seen him do times beyond counting . . . he smiled and raised his left arm in a friendly wave, at once acknowledging the voice and rejecting the question.

Then I heard the first pop. Later, everyone would say what people often say of gunfire: It sounded like firecrackers going off. I knew differently. I got a quick whiff of sulfur and my reflexes took over. I ducked, the only one who did, and then, as more shots went off, I hit the pavement and stayed there.

Most of what happened next comes back to me in freeze frames. I suppose we are indebted to television for that piece of language. But what happened, happened in microseconds.

When the shots stopped I bolted to the other side of the president's car but could not get in. The special locks on the doors had clicked into place and my mind went blank. I had forgotten how to open them.

I can no longer separate what I actually saw at the time and what I observed later in constant television replays. But a picture of the president's face is absolutely branded on my mind's eye, as he stood with his arm in the air and the bullets began spraying. He did not realize he had been hit. But the smile was gone. His face froze. There was a moment of hesitation, a look of utter helplessness.

Then Jerry Parr, a veteran Secret Service agent, the head of the White House detail, virtually dived into the president, bent him over to make him less of a target, and threw him facedown onto the floor of the limousine. When they sped away from the curb, Parr's body was on top of his, shielding him.

I ran to the next car and jumped in. As we wheeled in behind them, I looked out the window and saw Jim Brady and two others lying on the bloody ground. They were Timothy McCarthy, an agent, and Thomas Delahanty, a Washington policeman.

As we raced down Connecticut Avenue, other cars now following ours, I had no time to collect my thoughts, or my breath. I had assumed we were returning to the White House. The next thing I knew, we swung into the driveway of the George Washington University Hospital. It was twelve blocks from the Hilton. We made it in five minutes.

Parr had radioed the Secret Service command post at the

White House with the first report of the incident at the Hilton. His words were skeletal: Shots had been fired. "Rawhide"—the president's code name—was unhurt.

Actually, Ronald Reagan, who has a feeling that borders on hero worship for lawmen, for people who put their safety on the line, was mad as hell at Jerry Parr. He had been slammed so hard to the floor of the limo, he thought he had bruised or broken a rib. In complaining to Parr, I believe it is fair to say that he let out a curse word.

They had gone only a few blocks when the president coughed up blood. Parr could tell from the shade of red that it had come from the lungs. He instructed the driver to proceed to the hospital, and he radioed the command post of the change and asked them to alert the medical staff.

I leaped out of the backup car in time to see the president step out under his own power. He walked the fifteen yards to the emergency room, with agents on either side but not touching him. He moved through the door, out of public view, and then I saw him begin to sag. The agents caught him. His knees wobbled and his eyes rolled up. He was close to fainting, but still conscious. A paramedic lifted his feet and helped the agents, one under each arm, carry him into a private room off the lobby.

The hospital's trauma team was scrambling into place. As the door closed, I heard a doctor cry out, "Let's get some oxygen into him."

It is impossible to sort out all the emotions, all the confusion I felt at that instant. I was operating strictly on adrenaline. My first responsibility was to open a telephone line to the White House, and assure that a chain of authority existed.

At this point, it was still not clear that the president had been hit. The thought crossed several minds that he might have suffered a heart attack: His chest hurt. He was having difficulty breathing. He was a seventy-year-old man who had just suffered an attempt on his life.

In only the most disconnected way did the obvious questions run through my mind: Who, why, what? I had not seen a disturbed young dropout named John W. Hinckley, Jr., assume the police stance he had copied from television and click off six rounds in two seconds. From my vantage point, facedown on the cement, I had not seen the Secret Service men and hotel security guards, eight or nine of them, swarm all over him and take away the small revolver.

Struggling to stay calm, I got Ed Meese, the White House counselor, and Jim Baker, the chief of staff, on the phone and relayed what I knew: Brady and at least one agent had been hit. The president appeared to have a bruised rib. The doctors were examining him now.

Even as we talked, two ambulances arrived at the hospital almost simultaneously. They wheeled Jim Brady out of the first. McCarthy, shot in the chest, was in the second. The policeman, Delahanty, who had taken a bullet to the neck, had been delivered to the critical-care tower at another hospital.

While I waited for further news, keeping the line open, an intern in a green smock, holding a clipboard, approached me. He said, almost matter-of-factly, "Do you know who the patient is in the emergency room?"

I stared at him and saw that he was serious. I said, "Yes."

He said, "Would you give me his name, please?"

I said, "It's Reagan. R-E-A-G-A-N." I waited for a reaction. "First name?"

"Ron."

"Address?"

I said, "Sixteen hundred Pennsylvania."

His pencil stopped in mid-scratch. He finally looked up. "You mean . . . ?"

I said, "Yes. You have the president of the United States in there."

Baker and Meese, understandably, were anxious to reach the ·hospital. I asked them first to contact Mrs. Reagan and persuade her not to come. My relationship with Nancy was considered then, and is now, a special one. I did not believe the president to be in any danger. But people had been shot. There was a lot of blood. I felt it was not the right place for her to be, nor the right time.

But my message was too late. She had heard from the Secret

Service that there had been a shooting, and she was on her way to the hospital.

With the phone line open, I ducked into the room where the president had been taken. They had literally undressed him in seconds. I was stunned by the sight of my president, my friend, stripped, not a stitch on him, being lifted onto an examining table. One of the doctors had already discovered the small bullet hole in his coat, under the left sleeve.

Fifteen minutes had passed since I first put the call through. I went back to the phone with new and depressing information to pass on. "It looks like the president has been nicked," I said. And I now knew that Brady's wound was to the brain. I repeated what I had learned of the condition of McCarthy and Delahanty.

Even as I talked, Brady was wheeled right by me on a stretcher. I believe that was the closest I have ever come to passing out. They had removed the first dressing from his wound. His head was wide open. I know my voice was hoarse and strained as I told the people at the other end of the line: "It doesn't look good for Jim."

Things were happening so fast, it was so kaleidoscopic, I can no longer be certain which message reached which person in what order. I had sent word on the open line to my secretary to please call my wife and mother and let them know I was okay.

The most pedestrian of daily chores collided with the scary reality of high human drama. My wife, Carolyn, had taken her sewing machine in to be fixed at a shop in Georgetown. She heard the news on a radio. It was two weeks later before she remembered to ask about her sewing machine. She had just left it on the counter, unticketed, and dashed out the door. When she walked into the house, she picked up the ringing phone and took a call from my secretary, Shirley Moore, who had been trying repeatedly to call to say I was all right. Two hours had passed since the shots were fired.

Next, Carolyn raced to Blair's school and pulled our six-year-old out of class. She brought him home and turned on the TV. The first thing Blair saw was a videotape of the shooting. He saw Jim Brady pitch forward in replay after replay, and thought it was me. He sat quietly, in a kind of shock. In the confusion, it did not dawn on Carolyn that Blair needed attention or reassuring.

Of course, Jim and I have the same hairline, and at the time, I was several pounds heavier. That night, when I walked into my home after 10:00 P.M., my son threw his arms around me and clung to my waist. Only then did we convince him that I was alive and uninjured. Meanwhile, five or six of our friends had been sitting up with Carolyn. They were all praying—for Brady, for the president, for the two officers.

When Nancy Reagan arrived at the hospital she was still unaware that her husband had been shot. Gently, the doctors told her he had taken a bullet, but was doing well. They did not know exactly where it had lodged and were preparing to operate.

I studied her closely. She was near hysterics when they wheeled her husband to the operating room, and his first words to her were: "Honey, I forgot to duck." She leaned over and kissed him. A little of the fear and tension went out of the room.

By now Baker and Meese had joined me, and the president spotted the three of us. "Who's minding the store?" he asked. We laughed, the kind of nervous laugh heightened by concern. And then the orderlies wheeled him into surgery.

I turned to Nancy and said, "You know, there is a little chapel upstairs. Why don't we go in there for a while?"

So we did. Then we were led to one of the doctor's offices to wait and watch the news coverage on television. It was there that we heard the first mistaken report that Jim Brady had died. My mind had been turned in so many ways by then it was hard to react. The report did not surprise me. I had seen Brady lying in the street, and again inches away when they rushed him into surgery. I did not see how he could live.

At that point, the confusion was simply out there where the meter does not register. I thought that this is what it must have been like on November 22, 1963, the day John Kennedy was brought into Parkland Memorial Hospital.

The double doors to the emergency area kept swinging open;

patients on their aluminum carts were rolled in and out by teams of attendants moving briskly, holding the sides of the gurneys to keep them steady. Police were everywhere. Two or three times the Secret Service had to clear out the cops, just so the doctors could move through the halls.

Baker and Meese had found us, Nancy Reagan and me. We were still in the doctor's office on an upper floor, waiting for the outcome of the surgery. In the meantime, a matter of some importance had to be dealt with—running the country. I had put Baker on the line with Dr. Daniel Ruge, the president's personal physician, who described what was known about the wound: A small bullet had penetrated just under the armpit and Reagan had lost three or four pints of blood. Baker put down the phone and said his condition was "stable." The three of us looked at each other and nodded. The decision was made right there: not to invoke the Twenty-fifth Amendment, which would have transferred power to the vice-president, George Bush.

At the time of the shooting, Bush was in Fort Worth, Texas, speaking at a convention of cattlemen. He was to fly from there to Austin to address the state legislature. He was in the air when a coded Teletype message reached his plane, advising the pilot to refuel in Austin and continue on to Washington. The president had been shot.

The weight of those words humbled, and paralyzed, us. I pray to heaven we never hear them again. It begged the larger and once unthinkable question: Will the president die?

Finally, around 7:00 P.M., not quite five hours after the shooting, the president was delivered to the recovery room under an orange blanket. Through part of the surgery, Nancy Reagan had sat with the wives of Jim Brady and Tim McCarthy in an office on the hospital's second floor.

I looked in on the president while he slept. I was shaken by how bad he looked. His skin was gray and drawn, his breathing labored. I would go home that night and tell Carolyn, "He will never be the same." In the first photographs taken of him, after surgery, he looked like a corpse. I really thought the doctors, with their encouraging reports, were putting on an act. I couldn't have been more wrong.

Of course, I said none of this to Nancy. The thoracic surgeon, Dr. Benjamin Aaron, came out of the operating room and said to her, "It took me forty minutes to get through that chest. I have never in my life seen a chest like that on a man his age." The words were meant to be reassuring, a compliment.

I remembered what the doctor who operated on John Kennedy said, when he was asked what went through his mind as he prepared to cut open the thirty-fifth president: "He is a bigger man than I thought."

Of course, bigness is not in size alone. The popularity of Ronald Reagan, the remarkable acceptance of at least the first six years of his presidency, began to take shape that day, driven by his grace and aplomb under circumstances hard to conceive.

He did not leave the recovery room until 6:15 the next morning. We walked in on him—Baker, Meese, and I—half an hour later. He had a tube in his throat and could not talk without discomfort. The nurses were still buzzing over the notes he had blitzed them with, writing on a pad of pink paper.

One read: "I'd like to do this scene again—starting at the hotel."

After he had slept, and was conscious again, he dashed off a question: "I'm still alive, aren't I?"

And then a more profound thought: "Winston Churchill said that there is no more exhilarating feeling than being shot at without result."

He just would not stop. He was like an old trouper who had found the world's most appreciative audience, which in a sense he had. Another note read: "Send me to L.A. where I can see the air I'm breathing."

Not until days later did we realize that three of the notes were missing. Threats had to be made before they were turned in—by the White House staff people who had lifted them. Nancy has them now. They will become an exhibit when a Ronald Reagan Library is built—priceless, historical quips, written in the dawn after a dark night.

One of his 14-karat-gold cuff links, in the shape of the California golden bear, disappeared from his nightstand and was never found.

The tube was removed from his throat at three in the morning, and, now able to talk, he wondered about the attempted assassination. He said he recalled hearing three or four rounds. He asked if anyone else had been hurt. No one gave him a direct answer. It had been decided not to say anything that might, at that point, impair his recovery.

He had been hit, it turned out, by a fragment of a bullet that ricocheted off the armored car door. The bullet had pierced below the armpit, traveled several inches down his left side, bounced off a rib, punctured his lung, and come to rest three inches from his heart.

The attempts by newsmen to explain the medical details resulted in more confusion, and in a way added to the growing Reagan legend. Reporters kept saying he had been shot in the chest. Chris Wallace of NBC announced that Reagan had undergone open-heart surgery. Of course, he had not. The doctors had opened his chest to locate and extract the bullet.

When the three of us walked into his room, he was sitting up in bed, brushing his teeth. "I should have known I wasn't going to avoid a staff meeting," he said. When I tried to assure him that everything was going smoothly in his absence at the White House, he retorted, "What makes you think I'd be happy to hear *that*?"

We had brought with us a bill for his signature, cutting back on federal price supports for dairy products. It was just a wee step on the president's road to reduce the size of government, but it represented our first real legislative victory.

I doubt that many people realize now that Reagan had been in office just seventy days when Hinckley made his assassination attempt.

We asked if he felt up to signing the bill. It was not really a matter of any urgency, but all of us felt a pressure to demonstrate that the government—meaning Ronald Reagan—was able to function. The system had not lost or sacrificed its continuity.

He grabbed the pen and signed the legislation on his breakfast tray. The signature was weak and wobbly, and if I had seen it under other circumstances, I might have called it a forgery. But it was his. And the significance of that fact was not lost on any of us.

The gesture was symbolic. The president meant it to show that he was on the job. (There are White House secretaries who are able to copy his signature, and of the hundreds of letters mailed each day from the Oval Office, most are signed by an automatic pen. The pen is not used on *any* official documents.)

Reagan had been sheltered from newspapers and broadcasts, but that afternoon it was decided that he needed to be informed of the other injuries. The job fell to Dr. Ruge, who described Brady's injury as a head wound. The president asked him the question Ruge hoped would go unasked: Did it go into the brain?

When the doctor nodded, tears filled the president's eyes. He was silent for a moment, and then he said: "My God, that means four bullets landed."

Hinckley had been firing at nearly point-blank range. The weapon was a 22-caliber handgun, a Röhm RG-14, small but designed for accuracy.

The doctors had predicted that the president would need a minimum of two weeks to heal. He warned them he was a fast healer. He was out of the hospital in twelve days but needed three weeks, not two, to return to his desk.

The entire White House staff, and officials of the administration and their families, some two hundred people in all, were waiting on the South Lawn in a drizzling spring rain on the day the president came home. He raised his left arm in an easy wave, as he had done so recently in front of the Hilton, and I found myself flinching when he did. But of all of us who were there, I have a hunch that he was the first to put behind him the terrible pictures.

We had to persuade him, and ourselves, to limit his workday to a few hours until he was back at full strength. Nancy led the team, showing him a nice note she received from Lady Bird Johnson, recalling that Lyndon had needed a month to recover from his gallbladder operation.

Reagan confined himself to the family quarters, with an occasional excursion to the Rose Garden to catch the sun. His working schedule was limited to two meetings in the morning: with Baker, Meese and me, and with the National Security Council.

He sat with us in his robe and pajamas and was never self-conscious.

In truth, you could call on him most nights after 6:00 P.M. and he would be wearing his nightclothes. The Reagans are probably the biggest pajama fans this side of Hugh Hefner. On nights when he had a major speech or press conference, Nancy would order him to bed for an hour's midday rest at four. He said to me once, "I remember Lyndon saying he always took a nap in the afternoon. Must be something to it."

During his convalescence, the president received just one outside visitor, and the circumstances were unusual. On the morning of Good Friday, after we ended our staff meeting, he turned to me and said, "I sure would like to talk to a minister."

Nothing more was said. I was accustomed by now to such notions popping up, unpredictably. I went back to my office and called the Archdiocese of New York, and spoke to the assistant to Cardinal Terence J. Cooke.

The president had developed a relationship with the cardinal, one that may have been based initially on the pro-life connection. Candidate Reagan had attended the Al Smith charity dinner in 1980, honoring the first Catholic, a Democrat, to run for president. Jimmy Carter stayed away.

I told the monsignor, "I know it is Good Friday [one of his busiest days of the year]. But if there is any way Cardinal Cooke could get down here today, the president wants very much to spend some time with him."

Cardinal Cooke canceled his schedule and caught the next plane to Washington. I sent a car to meet him and bring him to the residence. Reagan led him into the Yellow Oval Room on the second floor, where heads of state meet the American president for the first time.

They sat side by side on a velour settee for nearly an hour, while I waited outside, fretting that the president might tire. As I walked in they were still deep in conversation, and I heard the president say, "I have decided that whatever time I have left is left for Him."

I waited a few seconds before interrupting, and then escorted the cardinal downstairs and out to the car. They would meet again several times in the next two years, the last when Reagan learned that Cardinal Cooke was dying of leukemia. He had kept his dreaded illness a secret until his condition could no longer be concealed.

When we heard that the end was near, Reagan called me in and said, "I want to go see him." That afternoon we flew to New York with Nancy and walked into the chancellery unannounced. The visit of Reagan was a surprise, not by our design but by the wish of the doctors not to excite the cardinal.

We were in time for the president to attend a mass in the chapel, and then went to the cardinal's quarters, where the cardinal was to give the benediction.

When everyone had settled into their seats in his study, Cardinal Cooke's eyes danced. "Ah, Mr. President," he said, "what in the world are you doing here? You are too busy to be spending time on an old man like me."

Reagan replied, "Well, you weren't too busy to see an old man . . . when you came to see me."

Cooke smiled. "I pray for you every day," he said, "and when I get to heaven . . ." He stopped and his eyes brimmed with tears. "Now that's a bit presumptuous of me, isn't it?" They both laughed, the sentence unfinished, the thought unspoken. A day or two later, we heard that the cardinal had taken a turn for the worse. Within a week, he was dead.

In his first public appearance after the attempt on his life, Reagan flew out to Notre Dame to receive an honorary degree. The audience gave him a sustained, standing ovation, as he stood with the cap and gown on, his face still drawn but with a smile that clearly said how grand it was to be there . . . to be anywhere.

On his return to Washington, he addressed the Congress, and walked to the podium amid a tumultuous welcome.

The public responded with sympathy to his brush with danger. But it was his refusal to dwell on it, the zest and humor with which he went about his recovery, that I believe gave Reagan what amounted to carte blanche in his first term—his so-called Teflon coating. It was, at bottom, respect and affection for a seventy-year-old man who thought nearly dying was no big deal. Living was.

In his quarters he started to exercise again. For years, in California, he had done calisthenics under the direction of a physical therapist. When he began his recuperation, his weight and chest expansion were down. He had the latest exercise machines brought into the White House and worked on them religiously. In a month, he had to have his suits remade. He went up a size in the chest, and the biceps in his arms just doubled.

Meanwhile, the question of protecting the president in a violent society was raised once more. And, again, it became clear that there was no way to guarantee his safety against an attack by a person crazed enough to risk his own life.

We resolved to do what we could to reduce the president's exposure to crowds. I would not forget, of course, that he had been hit while turning in the direction of a reporter's question. I knew you could no more stop a newsperson from shouting out a question than you can keep a rooster from crowing when the sun comes up. But from then on, I liked it better when the president did not stop for them. Which may explain all those TV clips of Reagan striding briskly from his helicopter to a car, signaling with his hand to his ear that he couldn't hear over the noise of the chopper blades.

During his stay, the hospital suite became a virtual White House annex. Nearby, special communications equipment was installed and a desk was moved in for his secretary, Helene Von Damm. We moved our morning staff meetings to the hospital's cafeteria, working over cereal and doughnuts. No one paid any attention to us in our blue business suits. Meese suggested that they thought we were doctors.

In truth, the government hardly skipped a beat during the president's recovery, in large part because of the Reagan style. He is a big-picture man who has never enjoyed immersing himself in details. And George Bush was superb at taking over many of the president's obligations, while avoiding the appearance of a man trying on a job for size. This was not, I believe, a political instinct but simply Bush at his considerate best.

At Cabinet meetings Bush sat in his chair, not the president's. He would not even allow a photograph of himself that included the White House or its offices as a backdrop.

Out of the madness of attempted assassination, and its uncertain aftermath, came a series of results far more encouraging than anyone could have imagined. Each of the wounded survived, and with the exception of Jim Brady, enjoyed full and normal recoveries. But even Brady has improved beyond what the doctors predicted.

When Tim McCarthy had recovered enough from his own surgery to be wheeled into the president's room, he received his commander's thanks "from the bottom of my heart." McCarthy, as the films confirmed, had put himself between Reagan and the assassin. "Someday tell your children for me," the president said, "what a brave man they have for a father." When he began to catch up on his personal mail, that thought found its way into a letter to the McCarthy kids.

In this experience there were fine moments of courage and compassion and gallantry. There was also one lingering embarrassment, involving Alexander Haig, which I regretted then and still do now.

I have always thought that the perception of Haig's performance, in the early confusion about the president's status, was largely unfair. I was then, and for some time, his strongest defender at the White House. This episode was not the reason for his departure from the Reagan administration . . . but it pointed him in that direction.

What had happened was this: While the president was down, the major figures in the government reported, as expected, to the Situation Room in the White House (code-named the Cement Mixer). There were Haig, the secretary of state, Caspar Weinberger, the defense secretary, William French Smith, the attorney general, and CIA chief William Casey. It was understood that Haig, as the senior Cabinet officer, should run the Situation Room.

They were assembled there in the event it became necessary to invoke the Twenty-fifth Amendment.

It developed later that none of the others had noticed Haig

leave the room. He had glanced up at a television set and heard
Larry Speakes, the deputy press secretary, answer a question
about whether U.S. armed forces had been placed on alert. The
reply seemed innocent enough: "Not that I'm aware." But Haig,
whose concern at the moment was properly with the reaction of
our allies—and our enemies—feared that the press might read
something else into the vagueness of that statement.

He grabbed Richard Allen, the national security adviser, and
decided to make an appearance in the White House press room.
With Allen at his heels, he ran up a flight of stairs and entered
the room unannounced, out of breath, his voice shaky, perspir-
ing from his effort. How Haig looked and acted did not exactly
inspire confidence, but possibly little would have been made of
what he said had he stopped with his first pronouncements: The
appropriate Cabinet officers were in the Situation Room, the
vice-president was on his way back to the capital, and no military alert had been ordered.

But when a reporter asked who was making the decisions, he
replied: "Constitutionally, gentlemen, you have the president,
the vice-president, and the secretary of state in that order, and
should the president decide he wants to transfer the helm to the
vice-president, he will do so.

"I am in control here in the White House pending the return
of the vice-president. If something came up, I would check with
him, of course."

I am in control here. Those words would haunt Haig. They
were slightly off-center, and at that moment seemed inappropri-
ate. But constitutionally he was dead wrong. The speaker of the
House, Tip O'Neill, and the president pro tempore of the Senate were next in line. And Weinberger, not Al Haig, was responsible for issuing emergency military commands in the
absence of the nation's top two leaders.

When Weinberger first saw Haig on the television screen, he
wondered why the network was running an old videotape of the
secretary of state. Then he looked around the room and saw
that Al was gone. The picture was live.

Back in the Situation Room, the two of them squared off and
angry words were exchanged. Weinberger was not only unable

to convince Haig that he had been in error on the line of authority, but the secretary of defense had already ordered a low-level stage of military readiness, which contradicted the assurance Haig had just given the media.

What undid Haig was his failure to collect himself before he went on national television. His instincts were right. He wanted the world to know that our guard was up, that the government was working. But he looked like a man about to crack. And he never did regain the stature he had won earlier as the man who held together Richard Nixon's faltering White House during Watergate.

Later, after the president's complete recovery was assured, I had to face in a personal way my feelings of guilt about Jim Brady. I could not escape the fact that I had shoved him into the line of fire. Although he began to make a surprising and steady comeback, he had a paralysis of the left side of his body. He had difficulty controlling his emotions, and in conversation would alternately laugh and cry. You had to reach over and touch his arm to bring him out of it. He underwent intensive therapy to regain the use of his arm and leg.

Six or eight months passed and I was still going entire nights unable to fall asleep. Carolyn insisted that I had to have help. She suggested that I talk to Jim's neurosurgeon, Dr. Arthur Kobrine.

It was Dr. Kobrine who had removed all of the damaged brain tissue, along with the bullets and bone fragments, in a six-hour operation. An X ray taken in the emergency room had looked hopeless. The bullet had entered Jim's head above the left eye. His arms and legs were moving when they brought him into the hospital, as if in spasms. The bullet, called a "Devastator" and containing a small explosive charge, had broken up somewhere inside the skull. The only good news was that the left side of the brain had been spared, the side that controls speech and comprehension.

Among his friends, the fear was not so much that Brady might not survive—he was off the critical list and out of intensive care in a week. The fear was that he would no longer be Jim Brady,

the best of companions and a man of generous humor. It was
Brady, after candidate Reagan had made his famous statement
that trees give off chemicals that pollute the air, who went flying
down the aisle of a campaign jet, pointing to a forest below:
"Killer trees! Killer trees!"

Brady had the respect and affection of the press. Once he had
just seated himself at a press breakfast when a reporter immediately hit him with a tough question. "Hey," he responded,
"whatever happened to foreplay?"

So carrying with me a clinging guilt, I went to see Dr.
Kobrine. He listened without a word, as I confided that I was
unable to deal with the feelings I had. Then he asked: "How tall
are you?"

I said, "Five foot nine."

He nodded. "Jim Brady is six feet tall. That bullet would have
gone right over your head and hit the president just about where
it hit Brady."

Still, it was, and is, hard for me to see Jim and think about the
pain and inactivity he has endured, the glad times he has missed.

It is fair to say that life at the top of the political pyramid
never again held the same attraction for me after the assassination attempt. After only seventy days in the White House, I had
new reasons to reflect on, and to appreciate, my twenty years
with the Reagans.

The President's Clothes

For someone who has made the best-dressed list, whose build is such that he looks good in ranch wear, Ronald Reagan's interest in clothes can best be described as sporadic.

He is, for example, partial to a topcoat that detective Columbo would not be caught wearing. The coat dates back to the end of his film career.

Once, while he was governor of California, he asked me to drop by the house to pick up a red polo shirt he wanted to wear that weekend in Los Angeles. He gave me very explicit instructions on where to find it: in the far left corner of the closet in the hallway by the front door.

When the maid let me in, I explained why I was there, opened the closet, and looked inside. I had no trouble finding the red polo shirt. It was the only article of clothing in an otherwise empty closet.

After Reagan was elected president, Nancy made it a point to upgrade his wardrobe, with the result that his attire today never has been nicer or more complete. Of course, she kept a sharp eye out to make sure he did not retrieve garments she had indexed for the Salvation Army.

In the continuing effort to replenish the president's clothes, Nancy discovered on one of our trips abroad a fine English tailor. Together we selected a blue and gray plaid swatch and sent the order to the tailor, who had kept his measurements on file. On the small swatch the pattern looked splendid. But swatches can be deceiving when they expand to become couches, seat covers for cars, wallpaper, or men's tailored suits.

When we eagerly opened the box from London, Nancy and I both gagged. Almost in unison, we said, "Oh, God, this will never do."

And, naturally, Ronald Reagan loved it. That suit became his favorite and he found it appropriate for any occasion. He was wearing it, again, when he boarded Air Force One, where Nancy—who had not seen him since he had slipped out of bed that morning—was waiting.

She put her hands on her hips and said: "Ronnie, please, I wish you would give that suit away. If you don't, I may burn it."

He appeared startled. "You don't like this suit?"

"I have told you so a hundred times."

He turned to me for help. "Mike, what do you think of this suit?"

I said, "Mr. President, do you want me to be honest with you?"

He said, "Of course."

I tried not to smile. "Around the office, whenever you wear that suit, everybody says, 'If he had to be shot, why couldn't he have been wearing that suit?'"

2
The
Ex-Actor

Let me tell you about Ronald Reagan. I mean, not as the press sees him, or the way the liberals or the conservatives think they see him.

Let me tell you about the Reagan I have known the past twenty years, starting at the very end of the respectable film career that first brought him to public notice.

I suppose I ought to admit right here that this will not include a recital of romantic escapades with shapely Hollywood starlets. The truth is, for an ex–movie star, tall and handsome, Reagan has never had a wandering eye. This may not make him exciting material for the gossip columns, or as interesting as some of our other public figures, but it does make Nancy Reagan happy.

As a political person, he is simply the most human among us. Sensitive to the feelings of others, leery of declaring victory whatever the cause or arena, and incurably superstitious. If he emptied his pants pocket you would always find about five good-luck charms that people had sent him. I am sure he reads his horoscope every day.

Of course, this is part of the contradiction. He believes in luck and fate and events beyond our control. Yet I have known few men more secure, as comfortable with themselves, or less vain. I do not suggest that he lacks pride or ego. He thinks a lot about how he appears to others. Whenever he received visitors in the Oval Office, or had to walk out to the Rose Garden, his back would be so straight it almost curved.

The key to understanding Ronald Reagan is to know that he has been underestimated all his life. My guess is that this judgment extends to his movie career, although I must confess that I never saw one of his pictures in a theater. I never actually admitted that to him, but if he reads it here I doubt that he will be troubled by this omission in my cultural growth.

At any rate, I did see *Bedtime for Bonzo* at Camp David, on my daughter's fourteenth birthday. And she loved it.

I believe I am licensed to discuss the underestimating of Ronald Reagan. My first exposure to him was in 1966, in the Republican primary for governor of California. I supported his opponent, George Christopher, the mayor of San Francisco.

I had been an ardent Barry Goldwater conservative, but a disillusioned one when that particular movement failed in the 1964 presidential campaign. I have always considered myself a pragmatic person and I wanted to win. George Christopher was a moderate with an impressive track record. I was not convinced that Ronald Reagan could win. He had become a favorite of the far right wing of the party, after his electrifying speech for Goldwater at the convention. But the political wisdom was that the California masses would never take him seriously.

I saw Reagan for the first time during the primary—we did not meet—in the lobby of the Ambassador Hotel in Los Angeles. I was struck by his healthy complexion. My immediate thought was, "My God, he has on rouge." I had never known anyone in the theatrical business. But I soon discovered that those rosy cheeks were his own.

Reagan was still a political novelty, his convictions not widely known. He had grown up in a midwestern household where FDR was virtually worshiped. Roosevelt was a hero of his, and a role model in his later approach to the American people.

Granted, there is in that admiration a rich contradiction: Ronald Reagan came to office vowing to dismantle the social system FDR had launched. Yet the answer was in his roots. He was a son of the Depression, whose father owed his job to the WPA. He would never say that he rejected Roosevelt's policy, simply that the country had—or should have—outgrown them.

He had no problem justifying his early support for this icon of the liberal faith. He is always quick to point out that FDR, in his first inaugural address, talked about less government. The sharp historical swing, he contended, came later, for Roosevelt, his party, and the country. Too, Reagan admired him as a professional: the voice, the delivery, how he moved people.

When I first suggested a weekly radio show, Reagan leaped at the prospect—over the objection of everyone else on the staff. All I heard was how static and dated the idea was, how hard it would be to sustain interest. But the memory of Roosevelt and his fireside chats made it appealing to Reagan. Starting in California, and continuing in the White House, Reagan's commentaries often made news. (More than we sometimes wanted, such as the time he said, into what he thought was a dead microphone, that the bombing of Russia would start in five minutes. Regrettably, the mike was open. The only thing that bombed was the joke.)

My own entry into the political process had been slow and roundabout. My parents were Republican partisans. I can remember being sent away from the dinner table for saying anything nice about Franklin Roosevelt. My father was convinced that FDR had ruined the world.

At twenty-four, I accepted a job as a field representative for the GOP, and helped organize a pair of successful state assembly races. Soon after, I worked on my first major campaign, the 1964 senate race of George Murphy, who in a sense would run interference for the political debut of Ronald Reagan.

Murphy's opponent was Pierre Salinger, John Kennedy's former press secretary. He had been appointed by Governor Pat Brown to finish the term of the late Clair Engel. Salinger had once worked for the *San Francisco Chronicle,* but otherwise his California credentials were thin.

Murphy, an old song-and-dance man, absolutely at ease in front of a camera, won the election in an upset. Murphy's stock had risen after a televised debate during which Salinger appeared nervous, distracted, constantly looking out the corner of his eye. What the audience did not see was Murphy, standing six feet away, off camera, very slowly tearing up his notes.

Twenty years later, Salinger covered the European summit for ABC, and we had lunch in Paris, at Maxim's. This was the first time we had ever talked privately. After lunch, he slipped a cigar out of his coat pocket and I could not contain a sly grin. "I have a confession to make," I said.

"What's that?"

"When you ran against George Murphy, I was a kid with the Republican party, and one of my jobs was to follow your campaign. Whenever you stepped out of a car at one of your rallies, I handed you a cigar." Out of courtesy or habit, he always jammed it into his mouth. Virtually every picture you saw of Salinger showed him with a cigar in his face.

"Why, you son of a bitch," he said, his eyes lighting up. "You know, to this day I can't refuse a cigar." He said he smokes Havanas, up to eight a day, at a cost of around ten dollars apiece.

I did a quick calculation. "That's thirty thousand dollars a year," I said.

"Yeah," he nodded. "That's what I do with my money from speaking engagements. Put it aside to buy cigars."

You can't get away with such stunts in a political campaign today. No candidate would accept a cigar, fearful that it might be poisoned—if indeed you could get close enough to offer him one. A Secret Service agent would probably take off your hand.

After Reagan was elected governor of California, I was invited to Sacramento to help with the transition. I stayed on to work under William Clark as the assistant cabinet secretary. When the new governor appointed Clark as his executive secretary, Clark brought me along as his Number Two man.

Nancy Reagan was really responsible for the long relationship that soon blossomed. Bill Clark felt somewhat intimidated by Nancy, and asked me to work with her on any personal matters related to the Reagans.

And so began what came to be known among the Reagan staff, and eventually the press, as "The Mommy Watch." I probably found the phrase more amusing than Nancy did. She might have been upset, if she thought it was true, this suggestion that anyone needed to be assigned the job of humoring her.

I am not sure how that job description should read, but Nancy and I hit it off from the very beginning. Ronnie Reagan had sort of glided through life, and Nancy's role was to protect him. She accepted almost total responsibility for their family and home, and at the same time remained his closest adviser in public life.

I have struggled more than once to explain to others, and to myself, how Nancy Reagan manages her role. It is not just that she knows or understands her husband as no one else does. Most wives do, or think they do. She has made him her career, and the White House did not change or enlarge her methods or motives.

For as long as I have known them, she has used her persuasion with care, knowing when and how hard to apply the pressure. If he resists, she will back off and return to that issue at another moment.

She has not gotten involved at all, it should be noted, unless there is a controversy around him, or he needs to be convinced that an action is unavoidable. She knows you cannot barge in and tell him he has to fire Dick Allen or James Watt or Don Regan; that someone he likes has lost his effectiveness or has ill served him. She will wage a quiet campaign, planting a thought, recruiting others of us to push it along, making a case: Foreign policy will be hurt . . . our allies will be let down.

She lobbied the president to soften his line on the Soviet Union; to reduce military spending and not to push Star Wars at the expense of the poor and dispossessed. She favored a diplomatic solution in Nicaragua and opposed his trip to Bitburg. Nancy wins most of the time. When she does, it is not by wearing him down but by usually being on the right side of an issue.

If Reagan senses that people are ganging up on someone, he will resist every time, well beyond the point when he knows the move is inevitable. How much is loyalty, and how much is a distaste for being pushed, depends, I suppose, on the particular case. If changing his mind is seldom easy, there is a quality about him that discourages many from trying. A Republican came up to me at a dinner in Oklahoma one night and demanded, "You *have* to get him to cut the defense budget."

I said, "I'm in his office telling him that five days a week. Why don't you go over there and tell him yourself?"

He walked over and slapped the president on the back. I heard him say, "Hang in there, Dutch."

At times, Ronald Reagan has been very much a puzzle to me. I had never known anyone so unable to deal with close personal conflict. When problems arose related to the family, or with the personnel in his office, Nancy had to carry the load. Literally, it was through working with Nancy that I came to know her husband.

I knew nothing about his movie career and little about the period leading up to his election as governor. As we became better acquainted, he told me how General Electric had hired him as the host of its *General Electric Theater,* and for a television series called *Death Valley Days.* That connection became a kind of safety net, into which Reagan leaped when the movie offers stopped coming. He became the company's spokesman as well, and in speeches to management groups polished the themes that would point him toward elective office.

He told me once that the lowest point in his life was when he played Las Vegas. He was not exactly down and out in Beverly Hills, but he had grown bored and needed to work. His agent booked him into a Las Vegas hotel as a master of ceremonies for the floor show.

I honestly had no strong curiosity about that part of his life, at least the down times, and rarely asked about them. In the early years I was more intrigued by the whole Hollywood business because I had never been around anyone who was that type of celebrity. I enjoyed listening when he felt the urge to reminisce.

Except in minor ways, he is unchanged since our introduction twenty years ago. I recognized immediately that he was not a man who put on airs. When we first met, he was driving himself back and forth from Los Angeles to Sacramento, in a maroon Lincoln Continental, giving speeches to the Young Republicans.

He opened up to anybody who walked into whatever room he was in. I do not believe he could have survived politically, to the point that he has, without people protecting him. He truly believes in the best of everybody he meets, which is a wonderful way to live . . . if a trifle unrealistic. He came to accept the conveniences of high office, but they were not among the things that mattered to him.

As much as anyone I have known, Reagan attaches himself to a cause rather than people. His 1964 speech is remembered by some as his Goldwater speech. But he praised the nominee little, nor did he savage Lyndon Johnson at all. What he did was make the conservative case, in terms no one could misunderstand: "A government agency is the nearest thing to eternal life we will ever see on this earth." And he closed it with a riveting appeal to the delegates in the arena, and the viewers at home.

"You and I have a rendezvous with destiny. We can preserve for our children this last best hope of man on earth, or we can sentence them to take the first step into a thousand years of darkness. If we fail, at least let our children and our children's children say of us we justified our brief moment here. We did all that could be done."

There are those who would have said, surely by 1986, that Reagan had run George Gipp into the ground. But this is the real Reagan, believing in the Notre Dame football legend, believing in the lines from the script, asking Rockne, or the voters, to go in there with all they've got and win just one more for the Gipper.

I was aware that the role of George Gipp was the best known of his film career. Certainly, "Win One for the Gipper" ranks among the most quoted lines in sports or politics. Trivia fans might find it interesting that Reagan was paid $2,667 for seven days of shooting. He was one of sixteen candidates for the part, but Dennis Morgan was the only other actor who actually tested for it. Among those who lost out in the preliminaries were William Holden, John Wayne, Robert Young, and Bob Cummings.

Film critics and old Notre Dame fans praised Reagan for having done his homework, pointing out how well he even affected

Gipp's slight limp. "Actually," he would explain, years later, "I had on new football shoes and they hurt my feet."

I began to travel with him around the state, and then around the country, the two of us alone. You develop a relationship when you do that. It was only *after* he became a candidate for governor that he agreed to travel by air. He had it written into his contract with G.E. that he would not have to fly. He drove or went by train. Planes were not exactly a novelty by 1966, but the Reagans would not fly on the same plane until the children were out of school. When Nancy went on the road with him, I had to charter two planes. They were keeping faith with a kind of 1950s idea that the parents of small children should not tempt the odds.

Reagan rarely talked about himself during our hours on the road or in the air. But after six months or so, I noticed that every time we took off on a private jet, he would stare out the window. Finally, I asked him: "Are you saying a prayer?"

He said, "Yes, but how could you tell?"

I said, "I thought I saw your lips moving. What are you praying about?"

"For Nancy," he said.

I troubled the thought no further. But I knew what he meant: If anything happened to him, he wanted Nancy to be all right, and to be there for the children.

Of course, all through that first term the perception of him was still that of an actor. Every time you picked up a newspaper, the reference was nearly always to "Ronald Reagan, the former actor turned right-wing governor."

Such labels seldom upset him. He was fond of his Hollywood years and drew on them in interesting ways. When we were alone, I would ask him what this or that actor was like. One day I read that Dick Powell had died, and I asked him if he was as nice a fellow as people had said. My interest seemed to surprise him. "Mike," he answered, "you're always asking me about these people in the movies. I can only tell you that the camera seldom lies. Dick Powell was a great guy. That's what came across on the screen. If a guy was a snot, he came across that way."

I was intrigued by this insight and felt it was a valuable characteristic for a politician to have . . . this confidence that one could project what kind of person one was on film and, of course, on television. I learned from him in this respect and built some of my own public-relations theories around the things that came so naturally to Reagan.

When you brought a movie or TV camera into a room with him, he was always fine. But the sight of a still camera made him stiffen in a visible way. I asked him about it one day, why the still camera seemed to make him edgy. He said, "It's because I can't recover from what the still camera catches." In short, there were no retakes.

He was a voracious reader and, as the pile of work he carried with him on our plane trips grew heavier, he would look with envy at the book or magazine in my hand. He once told me that when he was a boy, his mother had drilled this thought into his head: "You will never be lonely, Ronnie, if you enjoy reading." And so he read constantly. He is the kind of person who, if nothing else is available, will read the ingredients on an empty gum wrapper. He loved fiction, especially westerns, anything by Louis L'Amour or Zane Grey.

I once gave him a book called *Lords of the Plains,* about a cavalry officer posted to West Texas during the Indian wars. He talked about the book for days, quoting the descriptions of the terrain. His pleasure reading pretty much stopped when he became president. From then on, most of his reading was confined to briefing materials and technical reports.

He did find time to read and enjoy Larry McMurtry's novel *Lonesome Dove,* again a saga of the West.

Reagan has, in fact, a passion for western culture and art. He was elated when he learned that the White House owned a collection of paintings and sculptures by Frederic Remington. He moved several into the Oval Office. He had special shelves built so he could display a collection of miniature saddles, made available by Walter Annenberg.

His friends keep an eye out for pieces they think he might like. When A. C. Lyles, who produced many a cowboy movie, spotted a bronze by Remington of a boxer, in James Cagney's home, he ordered one for Reagan. It was Lyles who told us, in early 1975, that he had just met the governor of Georgia. Jimmy Carter, he predicted, was going to be the next president of the United States. Carter had not yet won a primary. I laughed and said, "A.C., that shows how little you know about politics."

It was in the California period that I began to understand that there was a Reagan mystique, that it carried a force of its own, and that no matter how you tried you couldn't pin it down. I saw Reagan run for reelection as governor by running against the government. He campaigned as if he had not been part of it for four years. I can't explain it either. I only know it worked. He touched feelings in people about the bureaucracy, and about the size and role and cost of government. And very effectively, he would lay that beast at the feet of someone else. He could get away with it, I think, because he is a believer.

I also think he has been fortunate in the kinds of people he has been able to run against: for example, Edmund "Pat" Brown, who at that point in his career had come to be known as a kind of buffoon. He beat Pat and then got lucky again and ran for reelection against Jesse Unruh, a stereotypical Big Daddy political boss.

Reagan was already using the line in California that he had not left the Democratic party, the party had left him. And the party did make it easy, consistently underestimating him, always managing to field one of its weaker candidates against him. All he would do in his career was win and win again, while the press kept waiting for him to be chewed up by the politicians.

It is clear to me that the influence of Dwight Eisenhower, rather than Barry Goldwater, as commonly believed, completed his conversion from FDR Democrat to born-again, conservative Republican. I honestly do not believe that Reagan's positions ever changed. He was no more moderate, and no less conservative, in the 1950s than he is today. What did change was the political shading of the people who ran against him, the kind of campaign required of him, and the comparisons that were drawn at the time.

His public life began when he was viewed as fighting left-wingers in the movie industry, in the McCarthy era. When he supported Goldwater against Rockefeller, he was typed as a right-wing extremist (a classification Goldwater himself soon shed). In his campaigns for governor, Reagan refused to reject the support of the John Birch Society. He put a fine distinction on the issue, insisting that he was not accepting their beliefs, they were accepting his. Whether he needed their votes or not, whether the decision helped or hurt, mattered little. In the primary, for possibly the only time in his career, he found an opponent running to the right of him. By not taking on the Birchers, he was protecting his turf, and that stand reinforced the popular image of him.

Perceptions change far more easily than people. When Reagan made his late entry into the 1968 presidential race, Caspar Weinberger, then the state party chairman, took an unusual step. He endorsed Nixon, who had become the "moderate" candidate. Later, I was amazed when Reagan, needing to appoint a lieutenant governor, asked about Cap. I said, "Governor, the right wing will kill you." The mention of his name brought on antisemitic attacks, a curious twist given the fact that Weinberger is not Jewish.

Here he is today, the secretary of defense, unyielding hawk, guardian of the Pentagon purse, sweetheart of the far right.

Reagan has the capacity, as Eisenhower had, for heading the government without being thought of as a politician. His ability to make the country feel good about itself was seen as Ike-like in his first five years in office. So was the detached management style that later opened the way to so much criticism.

I have a picture of the two of them, in Palm Springs, and it is startling to see how Reagan towered over him. Eisenhower could not have been much over five ten, but that aura of command made him seem a much bigger man. In the late 1960s, Reagan traveled to Gettysburg to spend a day with the general and seek his counsel. Later, Eisenhower told Holmes Tuttle, one of Reagan's closest friends, "This is one hell of a Republican you have here."

Oh, yes, some would apply to Reagan the line that was used to explain Eisenhower's popularity: "I like a president who doesn't meddle in the affairs of government." They both had the

smile, the impression of warmth. But many who served under
him found that Eisenhower's benign nature was mostly on the
surface. Reagan's goes to the bone. All anyone has to do is walk
with him from the family residence to the Oval Office, talking
about the most urgent matters of state, and watch him nodding
and saying hello the entire time to the gardeners tending the
lawns.

I have seen him in a limousine, with a senator or some other
VIP who had cherished the thought of having Reagan's un-
divided time. And Reagan would be looking out the window,
waving, all the while assuring his guest, "Keep talking. I'm listening to you." At some point, he would explain, "I think these
people want to see their president."

FDR inspired him. Eisenhower charmed him. But if I had to
drop Reagan into a category, I would look beyond the past half
century. He was more of a kindred spirit to Theodore Roosevelt, the outdoorsman, the individualist. Of all the presidents,
he enjoyed reading about T.R. the most.

The California years were ripe and fulfilling, and one of the
lasting benefits for me was meeting the winsome young woman
who became my wife. I was dating Helene Von Damm, Bill
Clark's secretary at the time, later Reagan's. We drove to the
opera one night in San Francisco, and she suggested we stop by
a party at the apartment of a friend of hers. The friend was
Carolyn. She had been working in the governor's regional office,
and shortly was transferred to Sacramento.

She walked into my office one afternoon and asked for a
raise. We had a freeze on at the time and I said, "I can't authorize a raise for you but I'd love to take you to dinner." I think
she would have preferred the raise, but I persisted. I thought
she was the cutest thing I had ever seen. I finally persuaded her
to see a movie with me, and I took her to *Planet of the Apes*.
She could not believe my taste in movies. But in about two
months we were married.

She was a California girl, orphaned and adopted by a wonderful San Francisco family. Her father, a devout Republican, was
delighted she had chosen someone in politics. Of course, until
1985 our entire married life had been spent in the service of the

Reagans. For all the excitement and opportunities, she had to share me with another family, and many of those years were hard for her.

My parents had scrimped and studied price tags and saved to buy appliances on a monthly plan. That life was the one I knew. I came to envy this about Ronald Reagan, not that he had money, or was indifferent to it, but that he never seemed to give it much thought. In all the years I have known him, he rarely carried more than cab fare in his pocket. Once, we had been touring Europe for nearly three weeks, and after a staff dinner in a restaurant one night I picked up a check for nearly six hundred dollars. I laid my American Express card on the table, and the president said, almost guiltily, "Here, let me get the tip." He whipped out his billfold and pulled out the only cash he had in there, a wrinkled five-dollar bill.

On that note, it may be in order to tell you a little more about Michael Deaver.

My roots were lower middle class, not unlike Reagan's. In that respect, from the beginning I felt an identity with him. My father was a Shell Oil distributor in Bakersfield, a small valley town in California. Ours was the last house on the block to get a television set. We used to go to someone else's home every Wednesday to watch the roller derby and wrestling.

Early on, I learned the meaning of the adage "I felt sorry because I had no shoes, until I saw a man who had no feet."

We moved for a short period of time to a little town to the east of Bakersfield called Arvin, a community of migrant farms. On the last day of school, in the fourth grade, my parents made the traditional call on my teacher. In the middle of the conversation they ordered me to go sit in the car. I couldn't for the life of me figure out what I had done wrong. When my father opened the door and slid behind the wheel, there was embarrassment on his face. "Mike," he said, "why didn't you tell me you were the only kid in that school who wore shoes?"

I didn't know I was. No one had said anything, no one had teased me or suggested I had shown up my classmates. But we both felt sympathy for the children who had less than I had, and for the teacher who didn't know how to tell me.

These were the years not long after the Oklahoma dust bowl, when the rickety cars and trucks rattled west to California, mattresses and worldly goods piled on top. They carried entire families hoping to escape the bleak poverty and the relentless dust, sleeping at night with wet rags over their faces.

This part of California was where most of the cars and trucks stopped and the families settled. Even into the 1950s, children as young as ten worked in the citrus groves for pennies a day. Okies came to be a derisive term, and the townspeople claimed that the first three words they taught their kids were: *ma, pa,* and *Bakersfield.*

We Deavers had what we needed and not much else. I can still remember my mother having one of those accordion folders in which you would put ten dollars for the laundry and fifty for food and twenty for the doctor. There was just not much there. A small inheritance from my grandmother, around five thousand dollars, later enabled me to take piano lessons and earn my way through college.

The piano in our home had been my grandmother's. Then my mother struck a deal with a local piano teacher: free lessons for my brother, Bill, in return for using our piano in his classes. I was then about four and a half and the keyboard drew me the way a magnet draws a hairpin.

One day, on his way out of the house, the teacher told my mother, "You're giving the lessons to the wrong son. Mike is the one who is in here all day, watching my classes."

I always had a good ear. Even today if you drop a dime I can tell you if it is an F sharp. It has been one of the blessings of my life socially, and one of the best friends I have ever had. The music is always there, the piano always responds. I know exactly what its reactions will be. I can trust it.

To this day, Bill half jokes, half complains, that a plant my mother kept next to the piano thrived when I practiced my lessons. When I went off to college it just withered and died.

When I was eight, and in public school, I developed nephritis, a kidney disease, and gained nearly ten pounds in a week. I had to drop out of school and was tutored at home. At that time penicillin was not available, and the only medication was sulfa drugs. I went on a rigid, low-protein diet. After eight months the doctor cleared me to return to classes, but with a disclaimer. He said, "Mike, I think you're going to be all right, but you have to understand that because of this disease, and contracting it at this age, you are never going to play football, never going to be athletic."

The piano was a substitute for that part of my life, for the attention I couldn't get at the things young boys yearn to do. I was accepted by a fraternity in college because they needed a piano player. I was invited to join the Bohemian Club, an exclusive club in the redwoods above San Francisco, because they needed a piano player.

I always held jobs before or after school. I had a paper route, worked as a soda jerk, a fry cook, dug ditches, read meters, was an offset printer. After college, after I went to work for IBM in sales and concluded that the corporate world was not for me, a buddy and I took off on a trip around the world. That was another part of my education.

We saved our money for two years, and stashed away about four thousand dollars apiece. I made eighty dollars a night playing the piano three and a half hours in a lounge in San Jose. I more or less lived on my tips and banked the rest. I had no real spending money and nowhere to spend it. In college, I would cash a check for five dollars and it lasted me a week. If I had a date on a weekend I cashed another. I believe my life-style at the time could be fairly described as frugal.

During one stretch I played the piano at something like fourteen wedding receptions. One was a Roman Catholic service, and their organist failed to appear. They kept delaying the ceremony, and when I arrived someone asked me if I could play the organ. I said I thought so. They said, "Well, you can't play Handel's Wedding March ["Here Comes the Bride"], the Church won't allow it. Try to come up with something else." They moved back the service another half hour while I checked out the organ. The only song I could play on it was "The Hymn of the Dakota Indians." Afterward, the priest, obviously pleased, asked me, "Was that Bach?"

During my senior year in college I thought seriously, if briefly, about going into the Episcopal priesthood. I was very involved in a parish near the campus. One day the priest called and said, "Mike, the organist is sick and we're having an all-male service. We're expecting Bishop Pike. Can you help us out?"

Separate services for men and women had been a church ritual, now used for the most solemn or special occasion. James Pike was a celebrity, in and out of church circles, whose life had been touched by tragedy. His son had developed a drug problem and committed suicide in London. A tormented man, Pike had gone into the Ethiopian desert after a vision had led him to search for his son's soul there.

The organ turned out to be a massive, pipe-iron instrument that wound around the horn, with two levels of foot pedals and four levels of keys, hundreds of stays and stops. I had never attempted to play an organ anywhere near that size or sophistication.

The difference between a piano and an organ, for anyone who plays by ear, is unsettling. You can sustain the tone on a piano with your finger or the pedal, but with an organ the sound stops immediately. I realized I was going to have to play the mass in an hour and the pipes seemed a block away from me.

I decided the only way I was going to manage it was to read the mass as best I could and play it by ear. My problem was that the sound came a split second behind my movement. I tried to get through it by stuffing cotton in my ears. Unluckily, the bishop who celebrated the mass stayed one beat ahead of me. For those in the pews, it had to have been an awful distraction, like watching an entire movie where the words and lips are out of sync.

Six months later, I encountered Bishop Pike in San Francisco. "Reverend Father," I greeted him, "I haven't seen you since you celebrated that mass in San Jose."

He searched my face a moment, then said, "Oh, yes, I remember you. You're the one who screwed it up."

Episcopal priests are rarely called father anymore. The title was once part of the distinction between the high and low church. At the time of my own interest in the priesthood, there

were even Episcopal monks and celibate orders. I became
friendly with an elderly brother in the Order of the Holy Cross,
who always wore the brown cassock, tied around the waist. One
day I noticed there were three knots in the rope and asked what
they meant.

He replied, "Those are the Three Ds. No dames, no dough,
no decisions."

My college chum Berger Benson and I made it through Europe and down to Africa, where we went on a safari, then flew
to Australia. The last leg on our way home was to be South
America. We never made it. In Australia our money ran out.
My friend wired home for air fare and I was left in Sydney, flat
broke. I landed a job playing the piano in the Roseville Returned Servicemen's Club, which was the equivalent of our
American Legion.

The wages were small, the tips nonexistent, and after food
and lodging I never had enough left over to pay my passage
home. Finally, the club in San Jose offered to prepay my return
ticket if I would agree to a six months' contract to play there.

Once home, I viewed this experience as a sign that it was time
to get on with the more necessary side of life, such as looking
for a real career. Some might argue whether the next move I
made qualified as serious work. But I accepted a position heading the Goldwater campaign in Santa Clara County and, for better or worse, and nearly always for breakfast, in 1962 I found
myself in politics.

I do not think it ever crossed my mind that I would spend a
major chunk of my life at this calling. Certainly in the middle
1960s, amid the turmoil of Vietnam and student riots and racial
violence, it never occurred to me that I would follow Ronald
Wilson Reagan to Washington.

By 1970 the country was undergoing great spasms of change,
and no one wanted to predict what role Reagan would play, if
any, in the troubled times still to come. He was reelected as
governor that year, and on the last leg of the campaign someone—it might have been Nancy—had a portable electric piano
put on board the plane. I could not escape my checkered past.

And after a while I didn't try. Once, forty or fifty Republicans from all over the country met on a ranch in Tubac, on the Mexican border, to go dove hunting. Other recreations included drinking, eating, and storytelling. At one point the party piled onto several chartered buses and rumbled into Nogales for lunch. The restaurant had a piano, and without much prompting, I sat down and began to play.

When we prepared to leave, one of the hunters was so caught up in the festive spirit that he asked the owner how much he wanted for his piano. The proprietor kept insisting he did not want to sell. It was probably the only piano in Nogales. But the guest told him just to name his price, and he did. We picked up the piano right there and carried it to the bus. Later, the buyer had it shipped to his ranch and I suppose it is still there.

In 1970 or '71, I accompanied Reagan to Little Rock for a governors' conference, and a large group of us went to dinner at one of the city's most recommended steak houses. A private room had been reserved in the cellar, and after a round or two of drinks some of the governors demanded that the management find a piano so Deaver could play. Sure enough, there was a piano—upstairs.

There appeared to be no way to carry it down the narrow stairs and into the basement. But as luck would have it, Coach Frank Broyles and his Arkansas football players happened to be having a team dinner there. About eight of those big grunts just lifted the piano and carried it downstairs. I played the night away. And I imagine that piano, too, is right where we left it.

All of this played a part in the bonding of my friendship with the Reagans. There is surely something universal about sitting around a piano in the shank of the night, with liquid refreshment at hand and the laughter of friends in the air.

We have disagreed over the years, Ronald Reagan and I, but rarely in anger. One such occasion came in 1972, after Spiro Agnew had been forced to resign as vice-president and the disintegration of the Nixon presidency had begun.

Reagan was a staunch admirer of Agnew, and thought him a fine man who had been poorly advised. He continued to support him after the charges of bribe taking in his days as the Maryland governor had surfaced and he had retreated in dishonor from public view.

At a staff lunch one day, attended by six or so of us, the governor was clearly preoccupied. He kept toying with his car keys. Finally, he blurted out, "Gosh, I talked to Ted Agnew last night and it's really so sad and so unfair, what happened to him."

I said, "Governor, if that guy was Pat Brown you'd be beating his brains out. We campaigned against that kind of stuff."

He said, "Dammit, you're wrong. He's a decent man."

I said, "I'm not arguing that. I'm saying it doesn't help you to defend this man when the world knows he did something unethical. He has admitted to very serious misdeeds."

Reagan had no retort. He simply cocked his arm and flung his keys across the table, popping me right in the chest.

He was always a good athlete and once portrayed pitcher Grover Cleveland Alexander in a baseball movie. I had to admit, the governor had a good arm and I admired him for it.

Gentleman's Agreement

In the summer of 1975, Reagan delivered a speech in the town of Cullman, Alabama, and Governor George Wallace was there to meet him, amid speculation over both their futures.

Wallace, crippled by an assassin's bullet in the last presidential campaign, paid a courtesy call to his guest's motel room. They met for an hour privately, at which point I cleared my throat and said, "There are all kinds of press outside. You gentlemen need to decide what you are going to tell them."

Wallace smiled. "Governor," he said to Reagan, "Ford is up there [in Washington] worried to death about what we're doing here. And Hubert [Humphrey] has probably wet his pants by now. I think we ought to keep them in the dark, don't you? We ought to just say nothing."

Reagan agreed. He walked out to the parking area and, for one of the few times in his public career, put up his hands, smiled, said "Sorry, no comment," and ducked back into his room.

Whereupon George Wallace wheeled himself to the front of the crowd and held forth for forty minutes, answering questions about whatever the two of them had discussed.

As an old showman, Reagan knew when someone had stolen his scene. But he was only sorry that he missed it. He enjoyed hearing Wallace talk, the colorful way he spoke. What he took back to California was a lesson in southern hospitality.

A relaxed Governor Reagan

With the Carters

The Troika: Between Meese (left) and Baker as Jim Brady looks on.

March 30, 1981: A footstep or two before the first shot was heard. I'm at his side; Brady moves toward the press.

Giving Prince Charles the guided tour

With Bob and Dolores Hope

With Mother Teresa (center)

By the pool, Carolyn and Blair consult a former lifeguard.

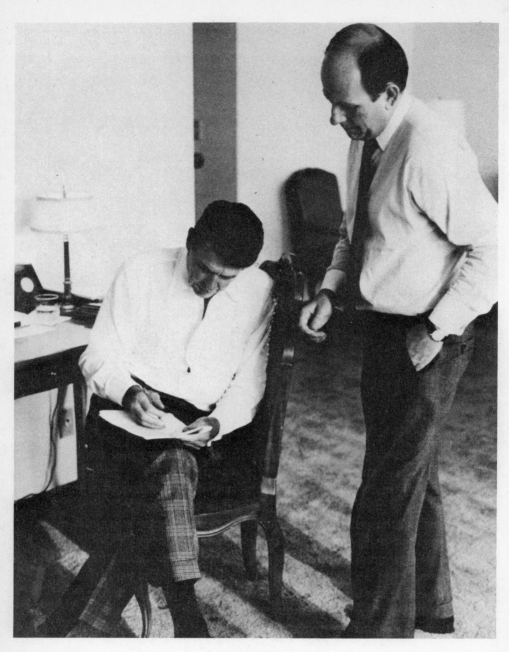

Paperwork

Aboard Air Force Two with Chinese Premier Zhao Ziyang

Meeting with Governor Wallace in '76

Canada's Pierre Trudeau has our interest.

3
The
Spirit
of
'76

I was not only with Ronald Reagan the year he decided to run for president, I was with him at the exact moment he made up his mind.

In January 1976, his terms as governor of California were two years behind him, and he had not yet given an answer to the groups clamoring for one. We were sitting toward the front of an airplane, flying from San Francisco to Los Angeles, when a woman he did not know stopped in the aisle next to his seat.

"Governor," she said, "you *must* run for president. You must do it for the people who believe in the things you do."

He had stayed out of the race four years earlier. In 1968, with the pros lined up with Nixon, and Rockefeller far behind, he jumped in at the last minute, virtually the week of the convention in Miami. It was too late to pull any significant support, but the excitement was there, and a glimpse of hearts yet to be won.

The measure of presidential ambition has been what someone once called "the fire in the belly." No one, including Reagan, really knew if he had it.

After the woman had left, he turned to me and said, "You know, she's right. Jerry Ford can't win and if I don't run I'm going to be like the guy who always sat on the bench and never got in the game."

I sat there, not certain whether to agree or disagree. Up to that time, I was still reluctant to express an opinion until he asked for it. But I was impressed with his motivation, this feeling that he had a duty to perform. I agreed that Ford could not win. I believed Reagan could, if he was able to communicate his ideals to the American people.

Then, as I had grown accustomed to his doing, he dug into his inventory of Hollywood anecdotes. "I remember in the movie *Santa Fe Trail,* I played George Custer as a young lieutenant. The captain said, 'You have got to take over.' And my line was 'I can't.' And the captain said, 'But it's your duty.'

"And that's the way I feel about this. I'm going to run."

I was amazed at how he had formed this titanic decision. Even as we sat there, he had worked it out in his mind. It was, quite literally, like threading film through a projector and at the end of the reel you had an answer. Up to that moment he had not said a word to me about which way he was leaning. Now I sat back in my seat, not ready to wrestle with the large plans that were waiting to be made.

Apart from the political implications, I was nearly as impressed with his memory of the film's dialogue.

From that moment on, I knew he was committed. The cynics may find it fitting that his inspiration came from a stranger on a plane, and a clip from an old cavalry movie. But that was, and is, Ronald Reagan.

The potential risks of his candidacy were not lost on any of us. Ford was a sitting, if unelected, president, and Reagan considered himself a loyalist, a consummate party man. No Republican president had been denied his party's renomination in one hundred years.

None had been challenged within the party since Teddy Roosevelt did so in 1912, against William Howard Taft, and lost.

Reagan had accepted as an article of faith the so-called Eleventh Commandment, the motto of the California party: "Thou Shalt Not Speak Ill of Other Republicans." A former state chairman, Gaylord Parkinson, had actually originated that line.

But Reagan made it his own, and used it in 1966 to defuse the attempts of George Christopher to focus on his inexperience.

I had seen Reagan grow in eight years, and the idea of winning the presidency was no longer strange to him. In 1968, he did not feel ready, or sure, and was reluctant to push too hard. Cliff White, an adviser in each of his national campaigns, said of him: "He has the high-school senior's attitude that you do what you're expected to do, but you're not supposed to vote for yourself."

Given his background, and his personality, it was obvious even then that Ronald Reagan was something new in American politics. He was at the opposite end of the scale from a Richard Nixon, who for so long had been the party's dominant player. It was Nixon who, in 1952, had ridden a train for three days, from Los Angeles to Chicago, every mile of the way tryng to persuade delegates to support him for the vice-presidency, over his fellow Californians Earl Warren and Bill Knowland.

No one could have gotten Reagan to spend three days on a train, much less hustle delegates along the way.

The contrast was stark, Reagan so open and comfortable with himself, Nixon tense and unbending. There is the funny-sad story of Nixon, taping a television interview with David Frost after Watergate, and attempting to make small talk during a break, asking: "Well, David, did you do any fornicating over the weekend?"

Yet no one admired Nixon more than did Reagan, who may have been one of the last public figures in America to defend him in the stormy final days of Watergate. While Henry Kissinger accepted the credit for the successes of that administration, Reagan always believed that Nixon was the foreign-policy master, the one with a strategic view of the world. It is not a widely known or well remembered story, but Nixon sent Reagan to Taipei in 1971 to defend his China policy to Chiang Kai-shek. At the same time, Kissinger was in Peking, secretly making the deal to recognize Red China and cut back our ties to the Nationalists.

One cannot imagine an assignment less appealing to a man with Reagan's convictions. But he went, and when he arrived at

the Summer Palace he was met by the generalissimo and
Madame Chiang. The old warrior was like a stone, looking
straight ahead, silently, as Reagan explained why the move was
one the United States felt it had to make. Finally, Reagan rose
and said, "I'm not happy about this and I know you're not
happy. But it was going to happen in our lifetimes, and it is
better to have it happen under Richard Nixon than Hubert
Humphrey."

The argument was that the opening to China would harm and
distract the Russians. And if Humphrey, the liberal, had been
elected president he might have abandoned Taiwan entirely. We
would still maintain relations, cultural if not diplomatic.

In 1972, Reagan served as Nixon's California chairman when
he ran for reelection. The phone rang in the governor's office
one afternoon around 5:30 P.M. Nixon was calling from the presidential yacht, the *Sequoia*. He was outraged because Reagan
had selected a certain congressman as his San Bernardino chairman. Nixon said, "How could you pick him? He's a jerk."

Reagan put his hand over the receiver and whispered to me,
"Who is this guy he's talking about?" In a nutshell, there was
the difference between them. Nixon was distraught over who
would run the campaign in a town of 75,000 people. And Reagan, who appointed the fellow, didn't know his name.

Names were not a strong point with Reagan. But if a name
escaped him at a reception or rally, he could get away with it.
He talked to someone with such sincerity that they felt certain
he remembered them. His most notable slip was at a White
House reception honoring the nation's mayors. As people
moved through a receiving line, he grabbed the hand of one of
his Cabinet secretaries, Sam Pierce, and said, "Good to see you,
Mr. Mayor."

Pierce, a black, had been the head of the Department of
Housing and Urban Development for more than a year. But it
became an anecdote, nothing more.

Nelson Rockefeller was another who had some difficulty with
names, but got around it by greeting most people with "Hiya,
fella."

In 1972, President Nixon had asked Reagan and Rockefeller

to be his chief surrogates on the campaign trail. After the governor told me he had agreed, I called Bart Porter, who was in charge of scheduling. I had one request to make: If Reagan ever needed to go from one coast to the other, in his role as surrogate, we would need a plane with enough speed and range to get him there and back in the same day.

The first time that situation occurred, I called Porter and asked if we could have the tail number of the plane for traffic control.

He said, "Yeah, I'll get it. The plane's a Lear."

My voice was icy. "A Lear? We'll have to make a stop each way for fuel, and he has to be back in the morning for legislation in Sacramento."

Porter's reply, in essence, was "Tough luck."

I said, "That's not good enough. He isn't going."

Porter said, "Wait a minute. He has to be there. He's the principal speaker."

When I hung up, I went into the governor's office and told him, "This may seem minor, but we have to stay firm or the Nixon organization will screw us every time."

Around ten o'clock that night, I received a call from Lyn Nofziger, who was working for CREEP (the aptly named Committee to Re-Elect the President). He said, "You son of a bitch, I've got a stretch DC-Eight for you. Is that big enough?"

The plane had seating for 280 passengers. Five of us were going on the trip. I said, "Bigness has nothing to do with it. My concern is the range. We have to fly to Miami in the morning and be back here that night. I don't want him to have two stopovers."

In Miami, we picked up two more passengers who had been on the program: Red Skelton and Pat O'Brien. By the time the plane leveled off, the drinking and the storytelling had started. I was in tears one moment, doubled over in laughter the next. Irish jokes, Hollywood stories, they were unending. O'Brien, in the title role, and Reagan as George Gipp, had starred in *The Knute Rockne Story*. I honestly believe they were both sorry to see the plane land.

It was during this time that I attended a meeting at the Century Plaza Hotel in Los Angeles to discuss Nixon's California campaign. The date was June 17, 1972. Jeb Magruder, John Mitchell, and Fred LaRue had flown in from Washington. A phone call came in for Magruder, who stepped into the next room to take it. Five minutes later, he came to the doorway and said he needed a private word with Mitchell and LaRue.

When the three of them returned, I asked Magruder what was going on.

He said, "Aw, some guys broke into the Democratic National Committee headquarters."

I blurted out, "Jesus, I hope your guys didn't have anything to do with it."

Magruder shrugged and said, "Nothing to worry about."

Reagan had proved to himself, during his years in Sacramento, that he could run the government of the largest state in the Union. How much harder could the Union itself be?

I did not get deeply involved in the strategy of the campaigns. My role, then as later, was to act as his confidant and troubleshooter. His campaign manager was John Sears, a skilled tactician held in respect by the press.

In some ways, 1976 was a model campaign, with less rancor and backbiting and meanness than most. Against impossible odds, Reagan stayed in the hunt, making a dramatic comeback after losses in New Hampshire, Massachusetts, Florida, and Illinois. At that point, the campaign was nearly broke and there was speculation that Reagan would drop out.

Two things helped us turn the corner. As Ford began to use the power of his office, distributing federal grants at various campaign stops, the governor agreed to suspend the Eleventh Commandment. Referring to Ford's recent appearances, he charged, "The band doesn't know whether to play 'Hail to the Chief' or 'Santa Claus Is Coming to Town.'"

The second factor was almost a fluke. A television station in Florida decided Reagan was owed a half hour under the equal-time rule. When his advisers were split over how to use it, Reagan himself decided he would give his basic speech. It was too late to change the outcome in Florida, but the tape ran, the money began to roll back in from around the state, and he scored an upset win in North Carolina.

The tape was edited for national showing and enough cash was raised to send us into Texas with a good head of steam. By now, Jimmy Carter had virtually sewed up the Democratic nomination. Lloyd Bentsen and George Wallace were gone, and the media attention was concentrated on the Republican primary.

Texas was Reagan country. A conservative state, pro-gun, pro-military, opposed to federal giveaways, and responsive to such stands as the one Reagan had taken on the Panama Canal: "We built it, we paid for it, it's ours and we're going to keep it."

I knew he would win after the papers printed a photograph of Ford eating a tamale with the husk still on it. Reagan shut out Ford in Texas, winning every county, every precinct, and all ninety-six delegates. Three days later, he won in Georgia, Alabama, and Indiana. He was doing well in the caucuses and conventions in the Mountain States. Suddenly, a contest had taken shape. Across America, Ronald Reagan was no longer on the fringe.

Ford was ahead after winning in Michigan and Ohio, his home territory. But it was clear that neither candidate had enough delegates to win.

Now the power of the White House again came into play. The two camps were virtually arm-wrestling for individual delegates, and there is hardly any tactic more persuasive than to have a telephone operator say "The President of the United States is calling."

Shopkeepers and librarians from small midwestern towns became overnight celebrities—if they were uncommitted delegates. We watched with blind envy as Ford invited them to the White House, and to join him on the deck of an aircraft carrier to watch the Tall Ships sail into New York harbor as part of the Bicentennial celebration.

Now how do you compete with that? An invitation to Disneyland, or even Dodger Stadium, somehow falls short.

In the Old West they had a saying: "It's time to call off the dogs, piss on the fire, and go home." We were nearly at that point when John Sears came up with a last resort, a desperation move that never before had been attempted. He urged Reagan to select his vice-presidential candidate before the convention, in mid-July. The sentiment was that we needed someone strong in the East who could break the logjam.

I really thought the plan had merit. In most cases, you spend so much time getting the nomination that you really leave little time for thinking about a running mate. It had happened to Hubert Humphrey in 1968, when he picked Thomas Eagleton without knowing about his mental history. It nearly happened to us in 1980. The idea of adding Ford to that year's ticket, with the inevitable references to a co-presidency, would have made a mush out of Reagan and his principles.

But now, in the summer of '76, on the eve of the convention, we were groping for a thunderbolt. The candidate had already proposed letting the nomination for vice-president be decided on the floor. The staff shot that one down on the grounds that it would be taken as a weakness, a cop-out on his first major decision. Next he suggested that we pick a woman—eight years before the Democrats did. "That," said Dick Wirthlin, his pollster, "would be more unpopular than picking a black."

Our immediate problem was that we needed to convince the eastern media, as well as the party power brokers, that the nomination was still open. The best way to do this was to press the idea that New York, New Jersey, and Pennsylvania were not locked up, no matter what the accountants said.

The name Sears recommended was Senator Richard Schweiker of Pennsylvania, at the time a Ford supporter, a Republican moderate, meaning that to many of the people most loyal to Reagan, he was a wild-eyed, bomb-throwing liberal.

The argument was that Schweiker could bring in Drew Lewis, his close personal friend, who headed the Pennsylvania delegation.

The initial shock gave way to curiosity and then to a sense of why-not-roll-the-dice? Reagan called Paul Laxalt of Nevada, whose border he had shared when they were governors and who was then Schweiker's seatmate in the Senate. There is no record, and no clear recollection of how the question was worded. But he asked Laxalt if Schweiker's views were compatible with his own. The answer was yes.

In retrospect, the answer seems odd. There was little about the public positions of the Pennsylvanian that would stamp him as a conservative.

In the end, the gambit failed, and even lost us a few delegates. Had it worked, the decision would have been hailed as inspired and shrewd. Losing, it came off as a gimmick, a cold-blooded political stunt. Still, it had been a shot in the dark worth taking, allowing Reagan to go to the convention with the press playing with numbers and unable to rule him out.

I will never forget a scene that took place as we labored to hold off a southern rebellion. Reagan invited Schweiker and his wife, Claire, a really lovely and gentle lady, to join him in a meeting with the Mississippi and Alabama delegations. After the initial pleasantries, an Alabaman stood up and said:

"Guv'nor, I don't know how you could have picked this fella. Ah'm not a drinkin' man, but the night I heard you picked Dick Schweiker I went home and drank a whole pitcher of whiskey sours. I would rather my doctor had told me my wife had a dose of the clap!"

And there, bless her, was Claire Schweiker, chin up, eyes unwavering.

Sometimes the hardest lesson in politics is not to take seriously anything anybody says about anybody.

About seven o'clock in the morning, after Ford had won the nomination, there was a knock at my door, next to the Reagan suite. I opened it to find Holmes Tuttle, Justin Dart, and William French Smith, part of Reagan's so-called California Kitchen Cabinet, all dressed in identical blue blazers and gray flannel slacks. They said they wanted to see Ron. I said, "He's next door, sound asleep, I'm sure."

They said, wake him, we want to talk to him about being vice-president.

I grumbled and argued that they ought at least to wait until breakfast. When they wouldn't leave, I dressed, knocked on our connecting door, and let myself in. I said, "Governor, Holmes and Justin and Smith are out in the hall and they think you should accept the vice-presidency."

No direct offer had been made, but the feeling was strong that only a signal was needed, an indication that he would accept.

Ronnie and Nancy whispered for a moment, then he said: "I don't want to do that. Tell them thanks, but no."

I said, "Governor, they are your friends, not mine."

With a disgust he did not try to hide, he climbed out of bed, slipped on his clothes, went out to the hall, and invited them inside. While they were talking the phone rang. He picked it up, said, "That's terrific. I think you made the right choice."

He turned around and said, "Fellows, that was Jerry Ford and he just picked Bob Dole."

I watched Reagan comfort his friends. It was dawn when they left. Around 10:00 A.M., he went downstairs to meet with the California delegation. There were his workers and his neighbors. He ended his talk by saying, "I want you to remember something. There is an old Scottish ballad that goes, 'I may be wounded, but I am not slain. I'll lay me down and rest a while and then I'll fight again.'" There wasn't a dry eye in the room, including my own. It was the only time in the entire '76 campaign that I broke down.

When Ford made his acceptance speech, I was sitting in a private box in the convention hall in Kansas City. John Sears and an old Eisenhower staffer, Bryce Harlow, found me and said Ford wanted Reagan to come to the stage and say a few words. I said, "No way. The press and the Ford people would say we were raining on his parade." I refused to pass on the message to the governor.

They pleaded. I said, "Okay, there is one way. If Ford invites him from the podium." On that condition, I had Reagan come to the box. He was sitting there when Ford finished his speech, looked up, and said: "Governor Reagan, I'd like you to come down."

As Reagan left the box to make his way to the stage, he said to me, "I don't have the foggiest idea what I'm going to say." Then he gave a brief speech that outshone Ford's, his "Shining City on a Hill" speech.

I am convinced that the convention in 1976 was the testing and the making of Ronald Reagan. It was his first defeat and, in losing, he won. He had made the turn toward becoming a credible figure on the national stage.

As we were leaving the next day, driving through town on our way to the airport, we passed a sign that read: REPUBLICANS, YOU PICKED THE WRONG GUY.

It was a sad trip back to Los Angeles, but the Reagans spent the entire flight going up and down the aisle, comforting everybody. The staffers were crying. Hell, even some of the reporters were crying.

I had been with Ronald Reagan ten years, working with him, for him, learning to read the small gestures that with this distinctive campaigner passed for moods. A lot of what worked for us was simply chemistry. Some of it was the fact that, unlike others of his advisers and consultants, I did not underestimate him, belittle him, try to elevate myself at his expense. It was popular, especially in the earlier years, to make sport of Ronald Reagan. Sears was a major offender. "He is an endorser," Sears wrote, after he was fired from the 1980 campaign. "Reagan sat with his California cabinet more as an equal than as its leader. Once consensus was derived or conflict resolved, he emerged as the spokesman, as the performer."

I am not sure Reagan himself would quarrel with that statement, as far as it goes. But he emerged as whatever he wanted to be. He saw the presidency as Teddy Roosevelt did, as a bully pulpit, and he understood that the laws, the rules, the new ethics have changed forever the perception of how the highest office in the land can function in the final quarter of the twentieth century.

It is early in these pages to be kicking around philosophy. But the Reagan Revolution succeeded, when it succeeded, not because this president told the people what they wanted to hear. He told them what *he* wanted to hear—and for most of America it was the same thing. He came to office at a time when the perception of what was done often mattered as much as what was actually done. These may be harsh thoughts, and not what the scholars and intellectuals and other wizards want to believe. But in the television age, image sometimes is as useful as substance. Not as important, but as useful.

This is public-relations chatter, up to a point, and I am not embarrassed by it. Neither is Ronald Reagan. His instincts in this area were unpredictable, but often effective.

In 1976, at the end of a long campaign day, I needed him to pose for a campaign poster that would be distributed all over the country. I picked a poor time. He was irritable, tired, snappish. "There must be ten thousand pictures of me in the files," he said. "Why in hell do I have to take another?"

The answer was that we needed a certain kind of photograph—a presidential one. Once past that hurdle, I zeroed in on his necktie. It was the pits, orange with a kind of inkblot, Rorschach-looking pattern. I said to myself, I gotta do it: "Governor, pardon me—but that's a terrible tie and you are going to have a picture taken that will be used in one hundred thousand reproductions. You need a nice, tasteful tie, sort of like the one I have on, blue with small polka dots."

He said, "I don't like *your* goddam tie, either."

I probably could have found a better way to put the request. He went to his quarters and returned in different neckwear, not much better than the first. His mood remained grumpy and the picture turned out poorly. We junked it.

In the long run, I think he had confidence in my judgment and knew I would do whatever I could to avoid embarrassing him. I learned early that he did not want to do things that were out of character. You might say to him, "Why don't you take off your jacket and sling it over your shoulder?" He would say, "No, I don't do that with my jacket."

Nor would Reagan ever allow me to plant a question at a press conference. Each time the issue came up, I would say that sometimes it was necessary. And his answer was always the same: "No, you can't hit a home run on a softball."

The meticulous care I learned to take in staging an event, down to checking the marks—where a performer stands—and camera positions, I picked up from Reagan. He would come out of a ballroom after making a speech and say, "Mike, don't ever let them turn down the house lights again. It causes me to lose my eye contact."

Another of his rules was not to set up the first row of tables or seats more than eight feet away from him. He wanted to be able to look at the faces.

Once, I tried to convince him he didn't have to sit through every dinner, he could just go in and make his speech. He said, "No, you'd be surprised how much I learn about my audience, watching them during the meal and the early part of the program."

Out of office, the next race four years away, Reagan turned to the task of consolidating his gains. With a Democrat in the White House, he occupied himself with a heavy speaking schedule, a syndicated newspaper column, and weekly radio commentaries. I became a partner in a public-relations firm whose principal client was Ronald Reagan.

He did what a candidate had to do: kept his options open. With funds left over from the '76 campaign, a political-action committee was set up to help other Republican candidates. Under the existing law, since changed, Reagan could have paid the tax and kept the money for his personal use. These candidates were for the most part conservatives, but in the mid-year elections of 1978, Reagan hit the stump for such moderates as Charles Percy of Illinois.

Reagan would turn sixty-nine around the time of the New Hampshire primary in 1980, but he was physically young. He made senior citizenship seem attractive, and no one ever figured out how to use the age factor against him.

He defused it by kidding himself, facing the issue rather than ducking it. His stock of one-liners included:

"You know, I've already lived some twenty years longer than my life expectancy was at birth. And that has been a source of annoyance to a number of people."

And: "I've been asked at times what it is like to sit and watch the late, late show and see yourself. I have one answer. It's like looking at a son you never knew you had."

And: "I can remember when a hot story broke and the reporters would run in yelling, 'Stop the chisels.'"

At a party for Russell Long of Louisiana, who was leaving the Senate at sixty-eight, Reagan wondered aloud why someone so young would want to retire. Then he told one of his favorite stories, about an elderly couple getting ready for bed:

"She said, 'Oh, I have a craving for ice cream and there isn't any in the house.' And he said, 'I'll go to the store and get some.'

"She said, 'Vanilla, with chocolate sauce.' He repeated it. 'Vanilla, with chocolate sauce.'

"She said, 'With whipped cream and a cherry on top.' He nodded. 'Vanilla with chocolate sauce, whipped cream and a cherry on top.'

"Away he went. By the time he got back, she was already in bed and he handed her the bag. She opened it and there was a ham sandwich. And she said, 'I told you to write it down. You forgot the mustard.'"

On the campaign trail, this candidate seldom forgot the mustard. Most of the 1976 team was back, with Sears crisscrossing the country and Charles Black working out of Washington. Drew Lewis, a dividend from our Dick Schweiker ploy, signed up early.

As one misfortune followed another in the Carter administration, the feeling grew that the next Republican nominee would occupy the White House. On our side, there was a disagreement on a central strategy. Sears argued that Reagan was the front-runner and should stay as much as possible above the battle.

In politics, one absurdity begets the next. Talk of "packaging" Reagan led to cries of "Let Reagan be Reagan."

Whatever those phrases were supposed to mean, I continued to fight to let him do what came naturally. It has become a cliché, but every time you get into any kind of political campaign you find these high-powered advertising people who want to stage the way Reagan delivers a speech: "Governor, we want you to walk around the desk, prop yourself on one edge, and . . ."

I would stop it there. "All I want is a talking head."

Without fail, someone would say, "You can't do that for thirty minutes."

"Not with most people you can't," I agreed, "but with Ronald Reagan you can."

I did not create the label The Great Communicator. I don't know who did. I only know that he ranks with FDR and John Kennedy, in this century, as presidents who could deliver a speech with the power to move people. He is, after all, a performer. The voice is pleasant, the confidence, the timing sharpened by thousands of speeches and scripts. And there is a sense entirely his own of what the moment may require.

It is an irony of these times that FDR, who stood for so many things Ronald Reagan later rejected, was the hero of his youth and the model for his own speaking style.

There is a misconception that Reagan has been isolated from the commonplaces of life. This was never true; even in the years when he seemed to pick his friends from among the wealthy and the successful, he was no elitist.

His problem with the press, if he had a problem, was his inability to deceive. What you see is what you get. Someone would come in and say, "Remember, Mr. President, this luncheon is on the record." The warning was an absolute waste of time. It made no difference. He was going to say the same thing whether the lunch was on or off the record.

When Reagan believes his truthfulness is being doubted, as in the case of the Iranian arms flap at the low point of his second term, his anger tends to rattle him. His lips seem to disappear. He may be flat wrong, he may embellish an anecdote, but he finds it inconceivable that anyone would accuse him of lying.

It may be instructive to look at the anatomy of a story from the campaign trail of 1980, how it developed and took on a life force of its own. This is a footnote on the road to Ronald Reagan's nomination, but it may give you an uneasy peek at life on the campaign bus.

Ten days before the New Hampshire primary, the candidate was passing time as he often did, regaling those around him with his inventory of stories and jokes. The state's top Republicans, ex-governor Lane Dwinell and Senator Gordon Humphrey, were sitting with him, at a special table at the center of the bus.

The bus was rolling toward Milford, on a two-lane road wet with fresh snow. Reagan was clearly enjoying himself. "Say, have you heard this one?" he asked. "How do you tell who the Polish one is at a cockfight? He's the one with a *duck*."

The air around him seemed to change. There was only scattered, strained laughter, which should have been a caution. But the candidate went on: "How do you tell who the *Italian* is at the cockfight?" Again, more silence. "He's the one who bets on the duck." The laughter was a little more generous. But the joke wasn't finished: "How do you know the Mafia was there?"

A few leaned closer. Reagan raised his voice: "The duck *wins.*"

The punch line brought a roar, and the circle began to break up. But among those listening was John Laurence, a correspondent for ABC News, who later wrote in the *Washington Journalism Review:* "I was astonished when I heard it. I thought Reagan had better sense than to tell an ethnic joke when he was running for president. Reporters were scrutinizing every move he made . . . tape-recording every word he said, probing his knowledge and searching out his thought processes."

At the next stop, Laurence and a few other reporters speculated on what the reaction would be if the story was used. We had a history of punishing official persons for tasteless or hurtful ethnic and racial stories.

But there were two drawbacks in this instance. To release the story now might seem politically timed; Reagan trailed George Bush in New Hampshire and the primary was close at hand. Perhaps more troubling, no tape recorder had been running at the time.

By late evening, the joke had made the rounds of the entire traveling press corps. Wayne King of *The New York Times* wondered out loud what might happen if he simply dropped a paragraph deep in his story, without calling any special attention to it, stating that: "Ronald Reagan told the following joke on the campaign trail today. . . ."

Gary Shuster, the Washington bureau chief for *The Detroit News,* was sitting with King. Shuster had covered Reagan's campaign in 1976, knew him better than most, and thought the joke harmless and not worthy of reporting. In fact, Reagan and the writers often exchanged jokes.

Wayne King continued to weigh the merits of filing it to the *Times.* Only the lack of any verification held him back. Only one reporter, Laurence, had been close enough to hear the words clearly. What if Reagan denied having told such a joke?

At that point, Shuster shrugged and offered, casually, to ask Reagan if he would repeat it. At 10:00 P.M., the bus neared its last stop of the day, and Reagan moved down the aisle toward the newsmen in back carrying a box of chocolate candy. This was a ritual courtesy usually performed by Nancy, who had left that day for an appearance in Chicago.

When the bus stopped, Reagan, with Ed Meese at his elbow, headed toward the exit and his last speech of the day. Shuster spoke up: "Governor, when you come back I want to hear that story about the duck." Everyone chuckled, including Meese, but to the surprise of the reporters, Reagan stopped in his tracks, turned around, and rattled off the story he had told earlier.

When the laughter died down, Meese piped up, "So much for the Connecticut vote." More laughs. Someone asked about the Mafia. "Yeah," quipped Ed, "there goes New Jersey, too."

Everyone laughed.

That night, in the hotel in Andover, across the border from Massachusetts, the reporters apparently could talk of little else. The phone lines stayed busy, writers and correspondents calling to test the story on their editors. Some were troubled mightily by the privacy of the first telling and the need to have Reagan repeat it for the press, a group that had included Don Oliver of NBC and Diane Curtis of United Press International.

A few double-checked the wording of the joke. King indicated that he planned to write the story for the *Times*. At the UPI offices, an editor gave Diane Curtis the go-ahead. Gary Shuster stuck to his original decision to ignore it.

The next afternoon, a Sunday, Laurence fed two radio reports to ABC News in New York, a total of less than two minutes, he said.

UPI piggybacked the piece about the joke with a slip of the tongue Nancy Reagan had made in her speech at a GOP dinner in Chicago. Quoting a phone conversation with her husband, in which he referred to the beautiful white snow in New Hampshire, Nancy ad-libbed that she wished he could be in Chicago "to see all these beautiful white *people*." Then she quickly tried to recover: "these beautiful black and white people."

The stories hit the air and the prints at nearly the same time, with the conclusion generally the same: that ethnic jokes made public have a way of backfiring on politicians who tell them.

The story did not appear on NBC, which carried instead a story on Reagan's foreign-policy positions, nor in *The New York Times,* where an editor spiked it.

Reagan was furious, feeling he had been taken advantage of and tricked. Much of his anger was directed at Shuster, who had not used the story at all, but who had requested the retelling. Based on the sequence of events, it would be hard not to conclude that Reagan had been set up for the benefit of the other reporters.

Now the process was in high gear. At virtually every stop, Reagan had to answer a question about the Duck Joke. He said he had repeated it in the friendly informality of the campaign bus so a reporter could get the order straight. It lingered as a story through February, but Reagan seemed to take the sting out of it during the New Hampshire debate. He said he told the joke only as an example of how awful ethnic jokes could be, and swore in the future he would tell only Irish jokes.

There was, in fact, a backlash and even the press seemed to rally to his side. In an editorial, *The New York Times* said: "Even people who detest ethnic jokes are apt to think Ronald Reagan is getting a bum rap. . . . Evidently, someone on the bus now feels obliged, with Spiro Agnew's clumsy 1968 gaffe in mind, to keep the Fat Jap vigil."

The reference was to a dreadful, thoughtless remark Agnew had made about a Japanese attorney on the staff of Senator Daniel Inouye.

Not for the only time, Reagan had the last word. In March, after feelings had cooled, he was flying to California on a Delta flight from Atlanta to continue the campaign. Among the other passengers, not a member of the party, was General William Westmoreland. They shook hands and the general said in a clear voice that carried back to a group of reporters, "I admire what you're doing. Keep at it." Then, as he walked away, he asked, "You're not telling any more ethnic jokes, I hope."

Reagan mumbled a meek reply, while the newsmen down the aisle could not keep from laughing. After Westmoreland had settled in his seat, Reagan looked around and called out to them: "You fellas are really gonna miss out, 'cause I know more than anyone."

He gave a sweep of his hand: "I mean, I know 'em all!"

Of course, the White House eventually hardened him. The political infighting, and the later, less charitable treatment from the media, chipped away at his eternal optimism. Yet few public men ever held on to their innocence as long. I marveled at him, traveling the country, as he watched all the newscasts, and read every newspaper he could get his hands on. He never looked at the front page first. He would turn instead to the comics, a childhood habit he never shed. We would land in a city and his reaction would be "Ah, Cincinnati, they have good comic strips here." Once, I heard him complain because a paper carried *The Wizard of Id* and you could no longer find papers that had *Andy Gump*.

In revealing such things, there is the risk of confirming the view of some of Reagan's detractors that he has been the Yogi Berra of politics. On the other hand, Berra appeared in more World Series than anyone in history, and is in the Hall of Fame, and many of his sayings have become part of the language.

In 1976, Ronald Reagan reestablished the principle that it isn't over until it's over.

Our Daily Bread

During the 1980 campaign, we had made a conscious decision to make our camp in the East rather than the West. We wanted that indentification, given the governor's California roots.

The Reagan staff leased a farm in Middleburg, Virginia, that had been owned by Bill Clements, then the governor of Texas. We were there one Saturday when Reagan ambled out of the house and said, "Mike, I'd like to attend church tomorrow. Is there one around here?"

I did some quick scouting and found a beautiful Episcopal church. I had a discreet chat with the minister and gently raised the question of what the topic of his sermon might be. He said he planned to talk on the issue of reborn Christians.

I coughed, explained that we had just left a convention in Fort Worth of Southern Baptists fundamentalists, and had heard what seemed like several thousand such sermons.

He pondered briefly and said, "How about Ezekiel and the bones?"

"Great," I said, and we agreed that the Reagans would attend the morning service at eleven o'clock.

We were not told, and I did not anticipate, that the eleven o'clock service would also be holy communion.

The Reagans belonged in Los Angeles to Bel Air Presbyterian, a proper Protestant church where trays are passed containing small glasses of grape juice and little squares of bread.

The Episcopal service is somewhat more formal, with kneeling and a common chalice and considerably more ritual. This kind of mass was very foreign to the Reagans and within minutes after we were inside the church they kept sending nervous glances my way. They were turning the pages of the prayer book as fast as they could, and I was handing them loose pages to help them keep up.

Nancy whispered to me in a mildly frantic voice, "Mike, what are we supposed to do?" I explained the ceremony as quickly and as confidently as I could: how we would walk to the altar and kneel, the minister would pass by with the wine (the blood of Christ), and the wafers (the body of Christ). He would bless them and keep moving.

The president, who as most people know has a slight hearing problem, leaned toward us but picked up little of what I was saying.

We started toward the altar and halfway down the aisle I felt Nancy Reagan clutch my arm. In front of us, all I could see were people crossing themselves and genuflecting. "Mike!" she hissed. "Are those people drinking out of the same cup?"

You have to remember that Nancy is the daughter of a doctor. I said, "It's all right. They'll come by with the wafers first. Then, when the chalice reaches you, dip the bread in the cup and that is perfectly all right. You won't have to put your lips to the cup."

The president said, "What? What?"

Nancy said, "Ron, just do exactly as I do."

Unknown to me, the church had made its wafers out of unleavened bread, which gave them the look and hardness of Jewish matzoh. Nancy selected a square of bread, and when the chalice came by she dipped hers . . . and dropped it. The square sank in the wine. She looked at me with huge eyes.

By then the trays had reached the president. Very calmly, and precisely, he picked up a piece of unleavened bread and dropped it in the wine. I watched the minister move on, shaking his head, staring at these blobs of gunk floating in his wine.

Nancy was relieved to leave the church. The president was chipper as he stepped into the sunlight, satisfied that the service had gone quite well.

4
Winning
the Rose
Garden

There is a cycle in politics, as in life, in which the weak grow strong and friends become enemies. And it works the other way as well.

Anyone who intends to spend as much as five minutes in an election campaign better remember those words. Or else never let your purse or your wallet out of your sight.

I have been fortunate in that the bad times were few, and far between, in my years with the Reagans. But one of them came at what should have been the peak months, when the goals were in sight and the rewards were just around the bend.

It was at my insistence that John Sears was brought back to head the 1980 primary campaign, over the objections of Paul Laxalt and other Reagan intimates. I still believed that we needed the eastern access that Sears could provide. I had a healthy respect for his tactical skills, and his calm, almost laid-back manner. A cherubic-looking guy, Sears was no ideologue. He was at heart a brain for hire who wanted to play on a winning team. And those were terms I understood.

But on any kind of campaign, the higher your rank the more likely you are to be dealing with egos, colossal egos, in what turns out to be a not very large compartment. Sears really wanted to run the show. He did not want to share power with anyone and, intellectually, he had little in the way of personal respect for the candidate he served.

No one had yet spoken these thoughts out loud, however, in the autumn of 1979. Reagan was seen as the front-runner, and the Republican nomination seemed to be his to win or lose.

I have to admit it. I got blindsided and I should have seen it coming. On Thanksgiving Day, Nancy called and asked if I could stop by their home in Los Angeles, in the Pacific Palisades, for a meeting. Carolyn dropped me off and Nancy met me at the door.

She asked if I would mind waiting a few minutes in the bedroom. I thought that was odd. I said, "The bedroom?" I glanced into the living room and there sat Sears, Charles Black, and Jimmy Lake with Reagan. I asked Nancy, "What's this?" She said, "We're just finishing up a few things. It will only be another five minutes or so."

Something was afoot. Nancy rarely sat through a staff meeting, or any other kind. She might drop in, or even be there at the start, staying just long enough to pick up the drift or to make a point. I sat and waited in the bedroom for twenty minutes and then I decided this was ridiculous. I walked into the living room and said, to no one in particular, "What's going on?"

No one looked directly at me, almost always a bad sign. Then Reagan said, "Mike, the fellows here have been telling me about the way you're running the fund-raising efforts, and we're losing money. As a matter of fact, they tell me I have to pay thirty thousand dollars a month to lease my space in your office building."

I was more stunned than angry. When Peter Hannaford and I had opened our public-relations firm, in January of 1975, our first client was Ronald Reagan. We had located the offices in West Los Angeles, close to his residence, partly to avoid his having to lease separate space and support a staff. There he had secretarial services, and a place where he could receive guests and conduct interviews. He was billed a pro rata share of the costs.

Now the plot thickens. In the figures he reported to Reagan, John Sears was quoting Bay Buchanan, who was then the campaign treasurer and kept the books. She was part of the Sears entourage, and a sister of Pat Buchanan, with whom I have fundamental differences. It is fair to say that Pat considers himself one of the last of the conservative purists. He once described me as the Lord of the Chamber Pot.

There may actually have been a month in which the Reagan campaign was billed thirty thousand dollars by Hannaford and Deaver. But that figure would have included, for example, four hundred dollars for office rental, so much for secretaries, advance men, limousines, and so many thousands for, say, a trip to China.

Reagan's average monthly bill, including for out-of-pocket expenses, was between five and ten thousand dollars. Someone had taken a thin tissue and constructed a high rise on it.

The charges never troubled Reagan as much as they did me. I was angry and frustrated and bitter, not because I thought he believed them, or that the question was raised, but that they would stoop to these lengths this late in the campaign.

All I could think was "If this is what these characters are going to do to me now, when nothing has been won, how far will they go if we end up in the White House?"

I made up my mind in that instant to get out of there. I said, with a self-control that surprised me, "You need to put somebody in charge, and if these gentlemen have convinced you that I am ripping you off, after all these years, then I'm out. I'm leaving."

I started out of the room and he followed me. "No, this is not what I want," he said.

I did not slow down. "I'm sorry, sir, but it's what I want."

I shut the door behind me and stepped out into the clean California air. I took a deep breath, looked around me, and suddenly I realized I had no car. I was stuck way out in the Pacific Palisades.

Feeling sheepish, a little like someone who had made a grand exit and walked into a closet, I slipped back inside in time to hear Reagan, standing in the middle of the living room, tell his guests: "Well, you sons of bitches, the best guy we had just left."

Nancy was only a few feet from me. I put a finger to my lips, a signal not to announce me, and asked in a whisper if I could borrow her station wagon. "I don't have my car," I explained, with a lame smile. Then I got the hell out of there, the car spitting gravel as I pulled away from the curb.

One of the things I learned that day was that insecurity rules the world. It seemed to me Sears feared my closeness to the Reagans. I went back to my public-relations firm and withdrew

into a shell for six months. I followed the campaign, saw it begin
to flounder, bumped into the Reagans in March, after he had
lost the Iowa primary, and heard from Nancy on the phone,
infrequently. Between March and November, we had almost no
contact. As a point of pride, I did not feel in a position to pick
up a phone and ask her how things were going. Of course, they
were constantly on the move.

In May 1980, with the race tightening and George Bush gain-
ing ground, Nancy asked if I would ever consider coming back.
She put it simply: "We need help."

I said, "Yes, you need Stu Spencer."

In another twist of the political blade, Spencer had given me
my start as a Republican field rep in 1964. By 1969 he hated my
guts, for reasons that were not clear to me then, and he had been
working for Gerald Ford. We had not really talked in years.

I began to hear from Nancy as it became obvious the campaign was stumbling. On the phone one night, she told me she
had come to the conclusion Sears had to go. He was not running
the kind of campaign in which Reagan—familiar phrase—would
be allowed to be Reagan. The perception in the media was that
Sears had emerged as a political guru and spokesman, and
Ronald Reagan was a kind of puppet on a string.

What Nancy said to her husband that week in the privacy of
their home is unknown to me. This much I know. She reviewed
for him the body count of people who had been his friends.
Nofziger was gone. And Deaver. Meese would be next. In her
usual way, Nancy had recruited Paul Laxalt and Dick Wirthlin,
associates of long standing, to call Reagan. They convinced him
that he had to choose between losing another confidant, Meese,
and this group of "Washington mercenaries."

On the morning of the New Hampshire primary, Reagan
called in Sears, Lake, and Black and said, "Fellows, this isn't
working." In language not much stronger than that, he let them
know their services were no longer required.

When I agreed to return, after Nancy had stage-managed the
firing of John Sears, my first moves were to recruit Stu Spencer
and to rehire Lyn Nofziger, whom I had fired.

We met for lunch in Los Angeles and each of us choked down
some pride. I said to Nofziger, "Look, Lyn, if I can go back so

can you." And the three of us came aboard that month for the stretch drive.

I had encountered Spencer while I was out of action, in the lobby of the New York Hilton Hotel. I was waiting in line to check in when I saw Spencer enter the lobby. He asked me what I was doing there and I told him, meeting a client. I gave up on the line and we went off to have a drink.

Four or five scotches later, I finally asked him: "Stu, we were good friends once. Why do you hate me now?"

He said, "I'll tell you why. In 1968, you obtained my confidential phone records and found out I was dealing with Albany [Nelson Rockefeller] at the same time as Reagan."

I felt a wave of relief. I said, "Stu, is that the reason?"

He said, "You bet your ass."

I said, "Then we can be friends again because it wasn't me." And I told him who had lifted the records, a guy he thought was his buddy (and a Reagan backer). From that day forward, Spencer and I have been the best of friends. As soon as he heard the name, it was as if a light went on. I should add, he has more than made up in the way of friendship for the long and needless freeze. At the height of the Iran-Contra fever, when the president was reluctant to move, and trying to ignore the calls for Donald Regan's firing, Spencer and I were on the same side. Nancy's side. We were a private channel to the president, bringing in opinions he did not want but needed to hear.

In politics, friends and enemies are sometimes interchangeable. I have taken steps on behalf of Ronald Reagan that were contrary to what a friend wanted, and earned myself an adversary. Those are the dues you pay for serving a president. In the case of Stu Spencer, and even now John Sears, old wounds have healed.

I rejoined the team in July. Bill Casey was the campaign manager then, and he asked me to come back as deputy director and chief of staff. At the risk of sounding too modest by half, I basically ran the airplane and supervised the advance work. I told Casey that all I wanted was to do what I did best, travel with Reagan and arrange the schedule.

In my absence, Bill Timmons, the deputy director, and Chuck Tyson, who had worked for me in Sacramento, had taken on those responsibilities. Three weeks after my return, I was called into Casey's office for a meeting with Timmons and Ed Meese. Casey said he had a problem, that Timmons had been promised he could be in charge of the advance work, and Tyson did not want to lose his title.

I said, "Yeah, you have a real problem, Bill. You made the same promises to me."

Meese, to his credit, spoke up and said: "Mike, they're yours if you want them."

I really did not feel the need to pull anyone's chain. I said, "Ed, I've had all the problems on this campaign that I care to have. You don't have to call me anything. I don't care what my title is, so long as nothing happens until I sign off on it, and the four of us understand that." They all nodded.

Tyson and Timmons got what they wanted, their squares on the organizational chart. I don't know to this day what my actual title was. I mean, we were talking about a two-month job that might involve the election of the next president of the United States. Of course, for those stakes priorities get tossed around pretty good.

But there was one question I had not bothered to ask. When I had left, my name had been right at the top of the organization chart. What good had it done me?

I was clearly uncomfortable on our first trip after my return. After we checked into a hotel in Peoria, Dave Fisher, a long-time Reagan staffer, knocked on my door and said the boss would like to have me up for a drink. I walked into the suite and he was waiting for me just inside the door with a scotch and water in his hand. With typical Reagan ease, he offered me a drink and said, "Where the hell have you been?"

I said, "Well, a funny thing happened to me one morning on my way to your house . . ."

Nothing else was ever said by either one of us about my leaving or my returning.

I like to think that my willingness to speak out, and my insistence on retaining a sense of personal worth, made me valuable to the Reagans. Nancy and I became a team, united by our shared belief that her husband needed to be protected, whether he wanted it or not.

In the latter stages of the election campaign, we were going out the door of a hotel in Chicago and heading for the airport, and I said, "You've had a good day. That was a good speech in there and that's the story, the one we want to run tonight on the news. So there is no need to take any questions when we get outside."

We walked to the car and as I waited for him to get in, he planted one foot inside the door and stood there and took a series of questions from the press.

When we had settled back in our seats and driven off, I looked at him in honest bemusement and said, "I don't believe you. I just don't believe you."

He said, "Why? What do you mean?"

"What you just did back there," I said. "I thought we had an agreement. You were not going to take any questions."

He brooded for a moment and then said, "Well, if you're so smart why don't *you* run for president?"

We rode the rest of the way in silence. Later that night, one of his assistants called and said the governor wanted to see me. When I walked in he handed me a slender box with a gold Cross fountain pen inside that someone had given him that day. He said, "I thought you might like to have this."

I knew it was his way of making amends, even if he still thought he was right.

No two days on the road with Ronald Reagan were quite alike. The press may not share that sentiment. They think they hear the same speech a thousand times, eat the same meal and stay at the same hotel in a different town every night.

But I never lost my capacity to be surprised. Of course, there was the running gag over his statement, in the Ohio steeltown of Steubenville, that trees also contributed to air pollution. We flew from there into Burbank the next day and you couldn't see the town below us, the smog was so thick. That morning when the campaign buses drove onto the campus at Claremont College, almost the first thing we saw was a sign hanging from a giant eucalyptus tree:

CUT ME DOWN BEFORE I KILL AGAIN.

One of the reporters was responsible.

And always there were the moments that were so ordinary they were to be savored. At a banquet in the Midwest, in a church, there were big bowls of country gravy on each table. When we got back into the car, Reagan mentioned how much he had enjoyed the meal. I said, "Yeah, I did something I hadn't done in years. I dipped some bread in that bowl of gravy."

A wistful look crossed his face. "You know, I wanted to do that, but I was afraid it wouldn't look too good."

It is probably worth noting that after several hundred state dinners, in the capitals of the world, his favorite dish is still macaroni and cheese.

There it is again: a man whose simple tastes are said by his enemies to match his intellect. That judgment has cost them many a victory.

In the end, it was a Reagan steamroller than ran over the rest of the competition in the Republican primary. Bush had been virtually knocked out in New Hampshire, in the famous scene in the high-school auditorium when Reagan invited other candidates to join the debate. Bush was not aware of the offer until the others, including Bob Dole and Howard Baker, approached the stage. Several conversations were going at once when Reagan settled the matter by announcing: "I paid for this microphone and I'll decide who uses it."

That clash took place during my time on the sidelines, but I have no doubt it helped turn the momentum toward Reagan.

Reagan swept Texas, the South, and the western states, and went over the top in the delegate count with two weeks to spare. The convention would ratify his selection on the first ballot.

In Detroit's Joe Louis Arena, Reagan accepted the nomination as the most conservative candidate since Goldwater. Yet his ability to hold an audience was never better shown than when he courted Gerald Ford as his running mate—and then decided on his most recent rival, George Bush. It was, to say the least, an unusual display of political showmanship.

At first, Reagan-Ford seemed the ultimate dream ticket. But nerves grew raw as the bartering dragged on. Again, Reagan demonstrated an interesting ability to stand back and observe what was happening around him. "When I first joined the party," he had said at a small luncheon that week, "I used to think the Republicans were people who would rather win a convention than an election. I think that has changed. We're focusing on the election now."

And so we were, which is one reason why the Ford idea had to be given an airing.

The mere fact that such a proposition was seriously considered reflects, I think, how flexible and open Reagan really is. Early in the week, a steady procession of high-ranking party officials and fat-cat contributors had filed through his suite, and most of them had Jerry Ford on their minds. I watched Reagan listen, and saw him react as I knew he would:

"Why not? These fellas all think he might accept if we offer it. What have we got to lose?"

This controversial proposal—asking a former president to run in the second spot on a new national ticket—served a variety of purposes: It made for fine theater, a gift to the television gods; it returned interest and suspense to what had figured to be a cut-and-dried convention; and it gave everyone a small sense of what it might be like negotiating arms reductions with the Russians.

From the start, I vigorously opposed the Ford gesture. Not because I feared it would smack of gimmickry, but because I considered it disastrous in every respect for Ronald Reagan.

There would be no end to the talk that he owed his victory to Ford, if he won. I did not see how we could have presented him for fourteen years as a man of principle and conviction, only to pair him with a former president best known for his compromises, whose policies he had consistently attacked.

But most of all, I objected to the talk of a co-presidency, or even a deputy presidency, and the bartering away of power that this arrangement implied. We were opening a Pandora's box, but the mood was so buoyant, the sweet smell of success so strong, everyone ignored that fact. There was no room, no time, to get the candidate's ear on this one. We simply had to ride it out. I thought to myself, this is like inviting the best man at your wedding to be the co-bridegroom.

The traffic in and out of Reagan's suite that week was like a Marx Brothers comedy. All we needed was the duck flying around the room. I hope I don't leave anyone out: There were Bill Brock, the party chairman; Bill Clements and Jim Thompson, the governors of Texas and Illinois; Henry

Kissinger; Alan Greenspan; Bob Dole, Ford's running mate in the loss to Carter; Congressmen John Rhodes and Bob Michel; and everyone with an aide or a pollster, so many GOP leaders we lost track of which side they were on.

And, of course, our people. Ed Meese, Bill Casey, and Richard Wirthlin had been named to "take a meeting" with Ford's people and exchange ideas. All this while, Jerry Ford was playing Hamlet.

I believe he wanted the job, saw it as a chance to return to Washington with honor and to redeem his 1976 defeat. In his heart, I believe he felt he could overshadow Reagan. Given his years in Congress, his friends on the Potomac, his special place as the man who had swept up the ashes of the Nixon era, this would not have been an immodest expectation.

On the other hand, Ford loved the life he now had: Having made the leap from being a man of modest income, for the first time he had all the money he could spend. He served on the board of a dozen powerful corporations. He had the Palm Springs life, all the golf his conscience could stand, and the freedom to go where he wanted and say what he liked.

I understood where Ford had landed. He had spent most of his years working for a paycheck. Now he had wealth and leisure and a wife happier than she had been in two decades. My own guess was that he would not give it up.

My man was George Bush. I barely knew him. But I saw him as a class person and I thought he would bring the right assets to the ticket. A moderate, with ties to the East (Yale) and the oil fields of Texas. The son of a former senator, Prescott Bush of Connecticut. Handsome, youthful, sharp.

The reference to Reagan's tax budget cuts as "voodoo economics" stung briefly, but didn't linger. Most of Reagan's men, myself included, appreciated it as a clever phrase more than a text on economics.

Now the games had begun. Ford wanted it. He didn't want it. He was wavering. He thought the idea was unworkable. He had reconsidered. He wanted changes. He had read the changes and wanted them clarified.

Meanwhile, back at the Pontchartrain Hotel, George Bush and his man, James Baker, were doing the only thing they could do: sit and wait. What made the waiting worthwhile, what produced the hope and excitement, was the inevitable feeling—on the convention floor, in the hotel lobbies, behind the doors—that Ronald Reagan would rout Jimmy Carter and become the next president.

The train was leaving the station.

Ford and Reagan met briefly on Tuesday and Wednesday. The conversations were friendly, respectful, and inconclusive. But the fact that Ford left the door open was taken as a positive step. And with each contact, Reagan liked the idea more.

In a room on the seventieth floor of the Detroit Plaza Hotel, Meese, Casey, and Wirthlin, possibly with suggestions from Bill Timmons, were drafting a two-page memorandum that would provide talking points for the two sides.

Ford wanted, among other assurances, a pledge that he would have a voice in Cabinet appointments. Two of the names mentioned were Kissinger and Greenspan. I don't think either name upset the governor. Of course, how his fans on the far right might feel was another matter. If that report got out, we would have probably needed to seal all entrances leading to the roof.

As the speculation mounted, as Ford consulted with his advisers and some of his supporters openly predicted he would agree to run with Reagan, television got into the act.

And confusion ran amok.

I was beside the candidate, and beside myself, as we watched the coverage on the big screen in his living room. The time ran out when Ford went on CBS at 7:00 P.M. to keep an interview with Walter Cronkite. And there, before a national audience of millions, we saw him openly discuss what was not yet decided, in details Reagan had hoped to keep private.

Ford acknowledged that an offer had been made. "If I go to Washington," he said, "and I'm not saying that I am accepting, I have to go there with the belief that I will play a meaningful role across the board."

In defense of Ford, I ought to clear up one statement that I believe was misinterpreted. The general impression after the interview was that Ford had endorsed the concept of a co-presidency. I don't think so. I believe he was trying to point out the pitfalls of it for Reagan. This is what was said:

Cronkite: As a matter of pride . . . it has got to be something like a co-presidency?

Ford: That's something Governor Reagan really ought to consider. Neither Betty nor myself would have any sense that our pride would be hurt if we went there as Number Two. But the point you raised is a very legitimate one. We have a lot of friends in Washington. And the president-to-be has to also have pride."

I took this to mean that Ford, quite correctly, saw the arrangement as a cheapening of the presidency.

As I had done so many times in the years (now fourteen of them) that had brought us there, I studied the face of the man next to me. He was stunned. His eyes sparked. He said, "This has gone too far. Get Kissinger on the phone. I want his [Ford's] answer right now." No one was sure how or when he involved himself, but Kissinger had emerged as the broker.

Frankly, Reagan was astonished. He felt he had kept his peace, had respected Ford's privacy and the delicacy of their negotiations. Now this.

By the time I reached Kissinger, it was pushing 10:00 P.M. He had by then appeared on TV, insisting that Ford's statements to Cronkite were "totally unpremeditated . . . by his advisers and, perhaps, by Ford." Now he told me that Ford had retired to his room and could not be disturbed.

I said, "Disturb him. The governor wants an answer now. This thing is getting out of control."

All three networks were running with the story. On CBS, Dan Rather announced that Bush had been informed of his rejection, a Secret Service detail had set up a ready room on Ford's floor, and before the night was over Reagan and Ford would appear jointly in front of the convention.

At about that time, Ford was making his way to Reagan's suite. They walked into a connecting room and closed the door, and my last glimpse was of Ford slipping an arm around Reagan's shoulder. They emerged less than ten minutes later.

When Ford had left, Reagan said quickly, "The answer was no. He didn't think it was right for him or for me. And now I am inclined to agree." Then he picked up the phone and said, to the amazement of everyone in the room, "I'm calling George Bush. I want to get this settled. Anyone have any objections?"

No one did, least of all me. It was interesting that he dialed the number himself. No assistant. No operator. Just Ronald Reagan reaching out to a former rival, offering him his party's nomination for vice-president.

Bush accepted . . . in five seconds or less. Then he swept up his wife and staff and piled into a motorcade to join Reagan at the convention hall. Along the way, they passed a police car racing to get Bob Dole and Howard Baker to the Detroit Plaza, for a final plea to Gerald Ford.

You could not have invented a more balanced ticket than Ronald Reagan and George Bush. One, a midwesterner, up from poverty, a performer, outdoorsman, and regular guy, strong in the West. The other, a child of wealth, of prep schools, a war hero—a commissioned navy pilot at eighteen—captain of the Yale baseball team, now a transplanted Texas oilman.

Bush had credentials where Reagan needed them most. He had served in Congress, as ambassador to the United Nations, as chairman of the Republican National Committee, as director of the CIA, as envoy to China. He was a professional who came across as earnest, well-bred, squeaky-clean.

The election had been rated a toss-up for months, but Reagan pulled away in the final two weeks and won it in a romp. I almost felt sorry for Jimmy Carter, buried under an economy that looked hopeless, whiplashed by our allies abroad and his party's own special interests at home. And, finally, consumed by the more-than-year-old humiliation of the Americans taken hostage by the fanatics in Iran.

Under the circumstances, everything Carter attempted in the campaign failed. He could not make Reagan look like a warmonger. Those who shared this fear were reassured by Reagan's words and benign television manner. For millions of others, the image of an itchy trigger finger was no liability. They were weary of seeing America pushed around. Reagan had it both ways.

The economy? Forget it. Whatever Reagan's plan, how could things be any worse than they were under Carter, with double digit inflation and 20 percent interest?

The age issue? Reagan had blown away half a dozen younger men in the primaries. He looked healthier than Carter. Jerry

Ford had gotten a laugh with the line "Reagan doesn't dye his hair. It's naturally orange."

But I swear to you, the hair and the color were and are his own. In all the time I was around him, he never dyed it. He did allow his barbers to leave the style more natural, softer and wavier, once he reached the White House.

My role during the national campaign was the same as in the primaries: running the plane and taking care of the candidate. My biggest irritation was his insistence on using Brylcreem. Yeah, exactly. He would put a little dab of it in the palm of his hand and rub it into his scalp. And he had a habit, before each press conference, of slapping water onto his hair. I begged him, "Governor, some people don't use that much water when they shampoo."

It was not until 1983 that Nancy and I finally got him off the Wet Look, the Brylcreem and water program.

I knew the race was won after the first debate with Carter, scheduled for 8:00 p.m. in Philadelphia. I had planned a quiet, early dinner, topped off with a 1964 Cabernet. I let Reagan have one glass of wine before the debate . . . a little color for his cheeks. The Reagans, Stu Spencer, and I were the only ones in the room. Then he went into the bedroom for half an hour to rest. When I walked in, to let him know it was time to leave, he was standing at the mirror, practicing his lines, rehearsing his opening statement.

On the morning of the inaugural, I arrived at the Blair House shortly before 9:00 a.m. to help the Reagans prepare for the ceremonies. When I walked in, Nancy was getting her hair done. I said, "Where's the governor?"

Without moving her head, she said, "I guess he's still in bed."

"In bed?" I repeated. "If it was me, if I was about to become president of the United States, I don't think I could still be asleep at nine o'clock on the morning of my swearing in."

I opened the door to the bedroom. It was pitch-dark, the curtains still drawn, and I could barely make out a heap of blankets in the middle of the bed. I said, "Governor?"

"Yeah?"

"It's nine o'clock."

"Yeah?"

"Well, you're going to be inaugurated in two hours."

"Does that mean I have to get up?"

Of course, people forget quickly, and the truth is that Carter and Reagan were neck and neck in the polls until the final weeks. Then, when it became clear that the hostages were not coming home, that there would be no October surprise, Reagan pulled ahead.

One of the things we had concluded early was that a Reagan victory would be nearly impossible if the hostages were released before the election. There was nothing we could do about it. We did, however, begin talking up the idea in August of an "October surprise." This had the effect of making anything Carter did before Election Day seem calculating and political.

Still, there is no doubt in my mind that the euphoria of the hostage release would have rolled over the land like a tidal wave. Carter would have been a hero, and many of the complaints against him forgotten. He would have won.

So there were even more than the usual wildly conflicting emotions at work on Inauguration Day of 1981. The president-elect, his family and closest advisers, walked over to the Blue Oval Room for the traditional coffee before we drove to the Hill. Carter was still in his office, in his shirt sleeves, his tie unknotted, working on getting the hostages out. It had become his obsession. His Great White Whale.

Carter's face was absolutely ashen, the color of the wall in my office (between gray and egg white). We spent only five minutes in the room. The mood was cordial but tense and awkward. No one said anything directly to Ronald Reagan, but the activity indicated that they would be working on the release of the hostages up to the last moment of the Carter administration.

Driving to the Hill, Carter and Reagan never really spoke. The outgoing president was on the car telephone the entire ride. He had dark circles under his eyes and it was obvious he had not slept all night. Reagan could see how much the timing of the hostage release meant to him.

The fifty-two hostages, members of the diplomatic staff in Beirut, had been held captive for 444 days by the followers of the Ayatollah Khomeini. Watching Carter, Reagan was troubled that any country could so manipulate an American president. The memory of that day makes all the more haunting the bitter irony of his secret arms negotiations, in 1986, with Iran.

When Nancy and Rosalynn Carter left to be seated on the platform, the governor—it was the last day I would call him that—took me aside. He said, "I have a feeling they are going to get the hostages back. If it happens, even during my address, I want you to tell me. Slip me a note. Interrupt me. Because if it happens, I want you to bring Carter up to the platform. I think it is outrageous that they are treating this president this way."

He was referring directly to the mullahs, and to the ayatollah, but also, I think, to the American voters who had turned with such a meanness of spirit against Jimmy Carter.

Twenty minutes after Ronald Reagan was sworn in, the news came that Iran had released the hostages. We had already left the platform, and the new president was having lunch in the rotunda of the Senate with the leaders of both parties. I passed him a note, and he stood and made the announcement.

Everyone in that room had goose bumps at that moment. But Ronald Reagan also felt a twinge of sympathy for the man whose office he had just taken. Later, he commented to me, "Did you take a close look at Carter? What a terrible day this must be for him."

On the morning of the first day I would go to work at the White House, I felt only exhilaration. I slid into the backseat of my chauffeur-driven car and took in every sight on the route. There was a bitter chill in the air, and as we neared the White House, I saw Jody Powell, Carter's former press secretary, walking along the sidewalk, kind of leaning into the wind, his hands jammed into his pockets.

And I said to myself, "Don't ever forget that, Deaver. You'll be back on the street someday."

Kiss of the Spider Woman

To most Americans, the Reagans remain a symbol of family values, so the polls tell us. The image does not quite square with the record. This is our first divorced president, a father who has suffered his share of rebellious children. Although only an occasional churchgoer, he has touched us on a spiritual level—more so than Jimmy Carter, who was as close as this country has come to putting a preacher in the White House. And that is not meant to belittle Carter.

In short, the Reagans are the most modern couple I know, yet still clinging to the values of the 1950s. They are role models to many troubled parents because they come across not as pious but as moral, consistently so. Which they are. Manners, morals, street language, all around us personal standards slide. The Reagans won't give in.

I once recommended to them a movie I had just seen, and was extremely moved by, called Kiss of the Spider Woman. *The stars were William Hurt, who won an Academy Award for best actor, and Raúl Julia. I did not attempt to describe the plot, knowing how distasteful it might sound. It was about a homosexual who is imprisoned in a South American jail, whose cellmate is a left-wing radical. The homosexual has nothing in life he desires except to give and receive love with another human being. The radical couldn't care less for that kind of love; for him life is a cause. His mission is to change the world.*

In the end, the radical discovers there is grace in giving of yourself—not necessarily in a physical way. And the homosexual finds that he is willing to take a risk for a cause, even someone else's. In the end, both die, the homosexual while trying to deliver a message for the radical.

I told the president I had seen a movie in which the acting was so powerful, they ought to order a print. They had one delivered to Camp David and watched it one weekend. Nancy could not wait to see me that Monday morning.

"Mike," she almost gasped, "how could you recommend that film? It was dreadful. We turned it off halfway through the reel."

"Once you get past the subject," I said, "it was an incredible picture."

She shuddered slightly. "How can you get past that?" she asked.

I should have known better. Both the Reagans are defensive about

what is offered on the screen today. The president has always re-
sented what he sees as the trend toward tossing out a four-letter word
just to get a rating. He points out, proudly, that he acted in the days
when "you could do an entire love scene with your clothes on. I
have always thought it was more suggestive," he says, "to see a hand
reach out and hang the 'Do Not Disturb' sign on the door."

5
The
First
Lady

While Nancy Reagan has always influenced her husband deeply, it would be a serious misjudgment to assume she does his thinking for him. They are not the Duke and Duchess of Windsor.

By that I mean he does not get his ideological strength from her. In many ways, the president holds to a harder line, is less quick to adjust and less willing to compromise than Nancy.

I returned to the White House one day, in the summer of 1982, after Carolyn and I had been to lunch with Lillian Hellman, the playwright, and Joseph Alsop, an elder statesman among political columnists. The two of them engaged in a very deep philosophical discussion about Marcel Proust, which I could not follow at all, and then Hellman said, rather wearily: "Oh, Joe, there is nothing left worth fighting and dying for."

Alsop replied, "Yes, there is, Lillian."

She said, "And what's that?"

Joe said, "The right to rule your own life."

I thought the president would be entertained by this anecdote. When I repeated it to him, he was puzzled, almost angry. "Lillian Hellman!" he said. "Dammit, she still thinks Joe Stalin is great."

Far left in thought, Hellman had been a hostile witness in the hearings that led to the Hollywood blacklist in the 1950s, and had lived with the mystery writer Dashiell Hammett, who went to prison for refusing to testify before the House Committee on Un-American Activities.

I knew Reagan was referring to that background. But I thought about his reaction for a long time. He and Hellman were about the same age, grew up in this country in the same era, moved in some of the same circles. At a time when Lillian Hellman went to the Left Bank in Paris with her parents, Reagan went to Hollywood. She saw that culture and philosophy, while he saw what he thought the West could provide: a society that grew instant millionaires, where a man can fly as high as his talent or hard work or luck will take him. He saw a certain kind of fame that attracted money and power, and I think that greatly influenced his life.

And I thought, They might as well have come from different worlds. Yet I often find myself drawn to the independent nature of a woman like Lillian Hellman, who wrote such classic plays as *The Little Foxes,* and *Watch on the Rhine,* and whose autobiographical works included *An Unfinished Woman* and *Pentimento.*

Nancy Reagan would have enjoyed that lunch, listening to other voices, the give-and-take of people with diverse views. As gregarious as her husband is, as much as he responds to good company, he doesn't need or seek it. He would be just as happy staying home and watching television.

His closest friends do not have sharply different philosophies. I often wished he had been more willing to expose his private self to opposing opinions. That he did not, relates, I think, to his sense of security and not, as his critics may contend, to a narrowness of mind.

I used to ask about his feelings, his reaction to all the things that were written or said about him. He can be in the same breath elegant and self-mocking, but he does not give back much introspection. It is almost as if he had figured it out years ago, certainly long before I knew him, and had no doubts about who he was. He has a 1950s concept of the world, has lived through the Depression and a world war and survived to enjoy an economy that gives people what they want almost instantly.

Once, when he was governor of California, there were just the two of us as passengers on a private jet. We were eating a gourmet lunch at 25,000 feet, and suddenly he said: "It really is remarkable, isn't it, what this country can produce."

He was caught up in the luxury of the moment. I don't think it occurred to him that fewer than 1 percent of the people would ever experience that kind of comfort. Yet he is not a man who covets anything, except perhaps a new tractor for his ranch.

I doubt that he knows what he is worth, or what his monthly obligations are. This is a couple whose finances, dating back to Reagan's movie days, always went through a business manager, agent, or lawyer. Everything was handled for them.

His suits and shirts are custom-tailored, but I have seen him in store-bought work pants he thought were terrific, and heard him rave over a Hallmark card he bought for Nancy. She would be just as touched if he brought her a card or a gold bracelet. Of course, what she wanted she would get.

Anyone who focused only on the image of Nancy Reagan, as it evolved from Junior Leaguer to Dragon Lady, missed her whole story. Her priorities started to change at midday, March 30, 1981. She became more independent, and patient, and less sensitive to criticism. This is how Nancy explained her reaction to the attempt on her husband's life:

"When you go through something like that, things that were important to you before, things that upset you before, they don't upset you so much. When I was in Sacramento, I used to go home and take a bath and have imaginary conversations in the tub with people who criticized me. And, of course, I was marvelous. I don't do that anymore. . . . I reached the point where I said to myself, 'I'm going to do what I want to do. There is nothing I can do about what people say.'"

She is revealed as well by the qualities that have not changed. Her self-discipline is unwavering. When she receives guests in the residence, on the second floor of the White House, she always offers them chocolate but never touches it herself.

There is the reflective Nancy, who can lose herself in a sweeping historical novel, or a thick biography, the kind that would break a toe if you dropped it on your foot. And there is the tender Nancy Reagan whose friendship has no price.

Not many people knew how close she was to the writer Truman Capote. They met through Jerry Zipkin, a lifelong bachelor and New York society fixture. A year or two before his death, Capote was arrested in Anaheim on a charge of disorderly conduct. Nancy called me at home and begged me to get him out of jail.

I asked her what he had done.

"I don't know," she said, "but you must get him out. It will kill him."

The fear and compassion in her voice were unmistakable. She could not abide the thought of this frail, lisping little man in a jail cell. I called Ed Meese, and he arranged for Capote's release.

It is their differences, as much as the many bonds they share, that I find revealing about the Reagans. The president relaxes easily, trusts everything, is beset by few doubts.

I want to be careful not to suggest that he believes in spirits. But Ronald Reagan does not laugh off paranormal phenomena. I no longer recall why, but we were chatting on the subject of superstitions one day in the residence. Abruptly, he said: "All my life I have had a recurring dream, that I lived in a house with high ceilings. I never knew what it meant. But I read somewhere that the Lincoln bedroom is haunted. Every once in a while, I'll find Rex [his dog] running down the hall and barking at the door of the Lincoln room."

I waited for him to go on, and when he didn't I said, "Well . . ."

The president said, unsmiling, "Well, it must be Lincoln's ghost he's barking at." I believe he was quite serious.

I doubt that Nancy Reagan, on the other hand, ever gets into a deep enough sleep to have dreams, mystical or plain. She is very intense, sometimes brittle in her manner, a compulsive user of the telephone. I always imagined that when I died there would be a phone in my coffin, and at the other end of it would be Nancy Reagan.

In the Oval Office, when the president referred to Nancy, he would usually grin and call her "your phone pal."

Friendships are to enjoy, not to analyze. From the outset, back in 1966, Nancy and I hit it off. It would not be far off to say the chemistry was right and leave it at that. But I believe she liked the fact that I did not try to sugarcoat the hard choices or withhold the bad news.

Nancy Reagan has been an easy target during much of her husband's political career. She struck the media, and through them the public, as a person of too many material possessions, always beautifully coiffed. She wore designer clothes, had wealthy friends, and enjoyed the social and high-fashion set. The friend most often singled out was Betsy Bloomingdale, whose late husband owned the New York department store. The press didn't know Betsy from a sack of potatoes, but she had the name and represented the glittery types Nancy Reagan was thought to prefer.

The timing of her decision to redecorate the White House gave her critics new material. It did not seem to matter that funds for the project, and the famous $240,000 set of china, came from private sources. The economy had not yet turned around, and her husband was proposing the severest domestic cuts of any president in history.

There were endless references to the adoring woman looking at her husband with glazed eyes. Not until the media began to see Nancy as a person, with her own strengths and interests, did that picture change. And then it changed radically.

Nancy Reagan benefited from a better public-relations effort, but that alone will not explain the transformation. Her staff kept trying to suggest causes or projects for her to support, and she kept rejecting them. She had been interested in drug and alcohol abuse in California, saw it now as a bigger national problem, and wanted to stick with that program. There was a risk that she would be seen as a dilettante, using a life-and-death issue to rehabilitate her own image. But her motives were real, and in the end people believed her.

Her work with the Foster Grandparents program also dated back to California. When the kids, Patti and Ron, began to need less of her time, she visited hospitals and retirement homes. She is blessed with the ability to be perfectly at ease around people who are maimed, disabled, or mentally disturbed. I have seen her walk into a room filled with mentally retarded children and pour her heart out. The kids would love to hug and touch her, attracted at first, I suppose, by her prettiness and the fact that she smelled good.

I have seen her sit and hold hands by the hour with a disabled veteran. When Nancy and the president met with the families of the victims who died in the crash of the Korean airliner in 1983, she took every one of them in her arms.

That scene repeated itself at Camp Lejeune, where she spent more hours comforting the survivors of the marines killed in the Beirut bombing. If anyone said something to the president, or made a move toward him, he responded. Nancy just naturally reached out and pulled them to her. She was absolutely bereft, yet she gave each person her strength.

I would prefer that these words not read like a revisionist history of Nancy Reagan. If the criticism of a public figure is out-of-bounds, praise will seldom balance it out. Besides, no matter how moving, these were private moments. The renewal of Nancy Reagan actually occurred in plain view of Washington's press corps and its media elite. She did an original and hilarious spoof of herself at the 1984 Gridiron Dinner at the National Press Club.

She walked out on the stage in rags, carrying a sack of cookies for her man, a Nancy no one had ever seen before. She was thin and distraught, not the Nancy with every hair in place. Then she sang "Second-Hand Clothes," a parody on the old song "Second-Hand Rose." There is nothing the press likes better than to see someone humbled or making fun of themselves. And that night Nancy turned them around 360 degrees.

I said to her afterward, "You were fantastic. How could you do it?"

She said, "Mike, people love it when you laugh at yourself."

Still, when the Press Club invited her to do the skit she agonized over it, consulting her friends and her husband, worried that she would not bring it off. At the end of her number, the audience was on its feet, the orchestra started up, and they brought her back for an encore. She could have done it over and over. I knew that she had turned a big corner that night.

Immediately after that she had a higher and more positive profile. She traveled around the country speaking against drug abuse, and was seen in public-service spots on television. She seemed to grow in confidence before your eyes. She understood, for possibly the first time in her life, that she could influence events on her own. She did not have to tag along and beam proudly upon her husband. Until that time, she would not have dreamed of having a separate schedule for herself, or appearing at the U.N. to talk about drug abuse.

She has even become much thicker-skinned about criticism. During her husband's first year in the White House, a critical column by Evans and Novak caused her to dissolve in tears. In December 1986, I picked up a newspaper and read a story quoting the president as telling Nancy, "Get off my Goddam back," about firing Don Regan. My immediate reaction was "Uh-oh, she is going to have a fit over this."

When I talked to Nancy later that morning, what she said was "Oh, that's not important. They have to write something about somebody every day."

Once, Lou Cannon of *The Washington Post* described her as "formidable" in a book about California politics. She was devastated. "That's a terrible word," she said. "Strong would have been much better."

When Chris Wallace reported that I had said the president slept at Cabinet meetings, I braced myself for Nancy's reaction. She shrugged it off: "We've all said things we wish we hadn't."

Her reaction to any adversity, anything she considers unfavorable, is to confront it. If she has a grievance with someone, sooner or later she goes directly to that person. If she regards you as a friend, and you disappoint her, you can always talk it out. Then it is over with, and five minutes later she may call back on a different subject.

I always knew when Nancy was unhappy with me. If I had not gotten a call from her in twenty-four hours, I would pick up the phone and say, "Have we got a problem?" If she said yes, I went right over. We might argue, but she never let me leave without a hug.

Most of the time I did not have to wait twenty-four hours. The president's health has been her main concern, just ahead of his place in history. My phone rang one day and she snapped, "I just received this week's schedule and I want to know what you think you are doing over there. You are going to kill him."

This is an area in which any first lady deserves to be heard. In spite of what was written, or what jokes were cracked about the president's work habits, overscheduling was a hard trap to avoid. I would get caught up in things and just keep adding events without deleting any.

Nancy's intensity is balanced by a sentimental streak. "Nancy," the president has said, "can puddle up when the laundry gets delivered." On the other hand, she is tougher on people than her husband is, much more demanding. She has been able, as a result, to develop around him a shield that allows him to be what he is. She will not tolerate sloppiness or stupidity, and he would.

Once a senator from a western state, a close friend of the president, failed to support him on a close vote. When the senator's wife called her on another matter, Nancy said: "I have to tell you, because I have to get this off my mind, I'm bothered by your husband's unwillingness to support Ron at a time when he needs him."

The next call Nancy received was from the senator. And the next day he was supporting the president.

Her directness, which troubles some people, has been an asset for Ronald Reagan. She has the ability to change someone's mind without giving up anything. So many people are never honest about what disturbs them. With Nancy, you rarely have to guess what is on her mind. In the same circumstances, the president would choke it down and say nothing. If a person tries to apologize to him, he will tell them he understands, even when he may not.

A myth grew up over the years that Nancy was responsible for the conversion of Ronald Reagan from New Deal Democrat to right-winger. Yet in Jane Wyman's divorce petition, she complained that he talked about politics at every meal.

His beliefs may have been influenced by Nancy's father, Dr. Loyal Davis, but the record isn't clear. If they talked about anything it was probably medicine. The subject fascinated Reagan. He could diagnose a brain tumor just by hearing the symptoms on a soap opera. A friend would mention a disease, and Reagan could recall word for word what Loyal Davis said would be the progression of it.

Reagan never really had a single political mentor. One who had an interesting view of Nancy's influence was John Huston, the writer-producer-director, who knew her as a very young girl. "She was the daughter of great friends of my father's," he once said. "When Nancy went out to Hollywood, she was sort of under my wing for a while, and then she married Ronnie. I'd see them occasionally. I love Nancy. I don't dislike Ronnie. I just disagree with his politics. I know one thing: The idea that Nancy is an archconservative and reactionary and that she is the influence on Ronnie and guided his political thinking is absurd, absolute nonsense."

Reagan is a strong man whose best personal qualities, his trust and candor and belief in people, have been taken for weakness in politics. Contrary to the belief that she moved him to the right, Nancy has been at her best in persuading him to take the longer view of history. When some of his staff wanted him to get tough with the Soviets, she argued that he should soften his language. What she saw was a man she knew wanted peace, who had been painted as strident and unyielding to the point of being a warmonger.

I know few professionals with a better public-relations antenna than hers. But many times Nancy will react to a problem by wanting to do away with the person who created it; or by simply trying to change whatever course or direction has caused her husband to be criticized. Would that the answers were always that simple.

If she makes a tenacious opponent, she is even more resolute as a friend. When Betsy Bloomingdale was going through the nasty times after a scandal broke about her husband, and Alfred Bloomingdale was in the hospital dying, Nancy was on the phone with her two or three times a day for weeks. She still has friends no one knows about, with whom she stays in regular contact, such as a woman who was in Auschwitz and Bergen-Belsen. I don't know how they met, but they have kept in touch for thirty years.

It is Nancy who does most of the gift buying, searching out the rare and thoughtful article, signing and framing the pictures. Her presents are nearly always something personal. Some of her old critics might be surprised to see her Christmas list, which included not only the Annenbergs or Sinatras of the world, but the fellow at the pharmacy, the barber, the people down the block.

In this society, people talk about true and enduring marriages the way an ecologist talks about the endangered species of the world. I have seen nothing to equal the depth of trust and affection between Ronald and Nancy Reagan.

For as long as I have observed them, the look, the touch, the feeling always has been there. When they moved to Washington from California, I was in Nancy's home in Los Angeles one day when she was wading through boxes and boxes of miscellany. At one point, she propped herself on a box and stopped to read a letter. Her eyes filled with tears.

The letter was from Reagan, written to their baby daughter Patti, while he was on a movie location in Arizona. It began: "Dear Patti, I miss you and Mom so much . . ." And the rest of the letter was about Nancy and what she meant to him.

When we were filming the eighteen-minute campaign documentary that would be shown at the Republican convention in 1984, I hit on an idea to generate a series of facial expressions I wanted from the candidate. I took about fifty photographs of events that had taken place during his first term, and had them enlarged. Then I had Reagan sit down and give me a spontaneous reaction as I showed him each photo, while the camera rolled.

There was one of Nancy carrying a birthday cake. He said, "Oh, I remember that, it was taken on my seventieth birthday."

I said, "No, what does that *really* mean to you?

He said, softly, without hesitation, "I can't imagine life without her."

Nor can I imagine one without the other.

I have heard people say their marriage cannot be what it appears, that no marriage is that blissful. Of course, it would be silly to imply that they have never quarreled, or had problems or serious disagreements. But I always thought they were the one couple I ever knew who never needed anyone else. They are simply each other's best friend.

Whenever Nancy leaves on a trip of her own, Reagan has trouble sleeping at night. He would drop by the Deaver or Jim Baker house in D.C. for dinner, or I would arrange for guests to visit and watch a movie with him. Anything to give him something to do.

Those who clash with her will perpetuate the image of Nancy Reagan as the Invisible Hand, manipulating, ruthless in dealing not only with her husband's adversaries but with friends who let him down. Let the record show that she acted, when she acted, only to protect the president. She does not set policy or attend Cabinet meetings or promote her own agenda. I suppose we have looked for that side of most presidential wives.

Nancy has worked hard to overcome the negative publicity of her first years in Washington: the frivolous, acquisitive first lady whose preoccupations were designer gowns and expensive china. For the first time, she has been admired for the person she is, and not just as Ronald Reagan's wife. Really, of the two of them, Nancy has made the greater stretch. She came to Sacramento tabbed as pretty much a country clubber, unprepared for the criticism they were bound to attract.

She is often described as the classic worrier, which is part of what makes them mesh so well. When he is off work, he is *off*. And Nancy goes on worrying about all the things he has put aside.

She has made sacrifices. The ranch means much less to her than it does to him. She goes, and stays a month, when I have no doubt she would rather be in Los Angeles with friends. The ranch is isolated, the house tiny and confining. I think, given her druthers, she would prefer not to spend hours a day riding a horse. But she continues to do it. She is a very, very disciplined person.

She is also a perfectionist. In most ways, she is much more like her adoptive father, the late Dr. Loyal Davis, than her mother, Edith, known as Dee Dee.

I would not think it possible to understand Nancy Reagan

without knowing this background: She was born Anne Frances Robbins, in New York City. Her parents divorced when she was two, and her mother, an actress, not unknown at the time, returned to the stage and to the road. Nancy went to live with an aunt and uncle in Maryland. She was six when Edith remarried, and she rejoined her mother in Chicago.

Where Ronald Reagan trusts everyone, except possibly the Russians and the Democrats, Nancy needs a lengthy trial period before anyone wins her confidence. There are conflicts in her that grew out of that uprooted childhood, the early absence of a father, and an adored mother who waltzed in and out of those years. But there was one towering compensation: In Dr. Davis she found the ideal father—Marcus Welby, only a bit more stern—and at fourteen she took his name.

Loyal Davis was a neurosurgeon, an authority figure whose students were frightened out of their wits of him. If one came into his office without an impeccably clean, starched white smock, or his shoes unshined, Dr. Davis would order the person out on the spot.

Her mother, who is still alive, edging up on ninety, is a lovely and boisterous woman who ranks among the best teller of raunchy stories in the world. Nancy could not, pardon the expression, say the s-word if she was standing in it. But Dee Dee would call me on the phone, as often as once a week, and give me a story to relay to the president. He and I would be holding our sides and Nancy wouldn't understand any of it.

Edith Davis had no qualms about calling anybody in the United States. She constantly called Mayor Daley, an old friend, and once rang up Lyndon Johnson, for what reason I would not even try to imagine.

She was beloved in Chicago, from the policemen walking a beat to the baseball players to the political bosses. She was a tiny, sparkling woman who would just walk into a room and light it up. Her devotion to her husband, and the contrast in their strengths, is reflected in Nancy's relationship with Ron.

Once, not long after I had gotten married, Carolyn took a call from Nancy's mother. When she routinely asked if she could say who was calling, Dee Dee let her have it: "I don't want to get into his pants, I just want to talk to him." She was, I believe, over seventy at the time.

Nancy wanted to be an actress, tried it, appeared on Broadway, had parts in eleven movies, and met Ronald Reagan. They were married by the time they co-starred in her last picture, where she played the role of his fiancée in *Hellcats of the Navy*.

I don't think she ever dreamed or thought about the kind of life she ended up having; certainly not a political life. I once said, if Ronald Reagan had owned a shoe store, Nancy would have been pushing shoes and working the register. And she would have been happy.

A key to Nancy is the fact that she is a wonderful flirt, in a genteel kind of way. She can charm the socks off anybody when she is so moved. At times she does it because she finds a person interesting; many times she will use this power for Ronald Reagan.

It was an education to see her turn up the kilowatts for Andrei Gromyko, the very stony and gruff Russian ambassador. He and the president had huddled in the Oval Office for forty minutes one day, while staff people kept insisting that they had to break for lunch.

Reagan, trying to be a sensitive host, showed Gromyko his private bathroom and asked, "Would you like to wash your hands?"

Gromyko said no.

Then Reagan asked again, "Would you like to use the facilities?"

Again, no, this time louder.

The president tried once more. "What I mean is, would you like to go to the toilet?"

And Gromyko said, "Oh, *da,* all right."

Finally, we made it over to the Red Room for light refreshments before lunch, and Nancy popped in for a surprise visit. She walked over to Gromyko, and for the first time, I saw him smile. Later, as he was leaving, he leaned over to her and said, "Whisper the word *peace* to your husband every night."

She replied, "I will. And I am also going to whisper *peace* to you every night."

With all this appearance of being formidable, of being the strength behind Ronald Reagan, she is more vulnerable than people think. She depends on him more than anyone realizes.

When there are political or family problems, Nancy tends to get uptight and emotional. In those times he is her rock. She has been torn by differences with Patti, torn between giving her daughter the independence she knows Patti craves and the feeling most parents have that space is another way of saying "leave me alone." Nancy was the one upset by Patti's novel, a *roman à clef* about a California political family. Reagan was hurt because Nancy was hurt. Nearly a year passed before they made their peace, at the president's request.

Maureen and Michael, his daughter and adopted son from his first marriage to Jane Wyman, were adults by the time I met the Reagans. But I was on the near sideline as Patti and Ron junior grew up, and I saw the pride and love and concern their parents felt for them.

When Patti was fifteen or sixteen and visiting our home one day, she was already complaining about her life as the child of famous parents. Finally, Carolyn said, "Patti, you can't have it both ways. You can't accept the opportunities they provide, and reject the obligations they have to meet."

Patti felt even then that she had too much supervision and too little control. She had a father who believed in marriage, the military, haircuts, and discipline, at a time when many campuses were aflame and young people were questioning all the old virtues. Her grievances were not original, but that made them no less real to her.

She worried about what would happen if she had a career as a singer or actress; would she be judged on her talent or who her parents were? She needn't have worried.

I don't believe children can go through life blaming their parents for every bump in the road. Maureen felt neglected, her distance from her parents growing as her father followed his political goals. But she neither lacked for love nor was smothered by it.

Ron was always artistic, with a gift for writing. His parents wanted him to finish college. He attended Yale for a year, then went to work in Los Angeles at the May Company, and announced his plan to take up ballet. The Reagans could have said, as some parents would have, that he should have started at ten, not eighteen, and he had lost critical years.

Instead they gave him all the help and encouragement they could. Nancy raised half a million dollars herself for the Joffrey Ballet, and Ron turned out to be one of its rising stars. Once he proved he could do it, he had achieved what he needed. He no longer wanted to commit to this art the time it demanded. He retired, married a lovely girl, Doria, and embarked on a promising career as a writer.

Ron takes after his father in many ways. He is sensitive and caring, but very secure about himself. He enjoyed his work, whether it was dancing or writing. I get the impression that he knows who he is, and he doesn't need to be famous or acclaimed to be happy.

Nancy knew what both Patti and Ron were going through, even if none of them could quite get the words across. As a young actress, wanting to be more like her mother, who was so sure of herself and made friends so easily, Nancy lived alone in New York in her twenties. Edith had an old friend call and stop by the apartment and take her out to dinner. The friend's name was Clark Gable.

No one would describe Nancy Reagan as star-struck, but she has a far keener sense of fame than her husband has. In their Hollywood years, they seldom partied, preferring to stay home and watch movies on their projector. Dinner out was usually at Chasen's. Nancy told me a story about a night in, say, 1959 and a stunning blonde a few booths away, around whom there was constant traffic and attention.

Driving home, Reagan looked up from the wheel and asked, idly, "Who was that beautiful girl everyone was fussing over?"

Nancy did a double-take. "Ron," she said, "I don't believe you."

"No, really," he said, "who was she?"

"Marilyn Monroe," Nancy answered, with a giggle.

It would be fair to say that Nancy has the stronger curiosity of the two of them. She is more aware of the finer things and of the subtleties of human nature. She enjoys reaching out to new people of whatever political coloring.

In my own time in Washington, I have been treated in some ways more generously by Democrats than Republicans. I became friends with the likes of Tip O'Neill, Bob Strauss, and Kay Graham. The way I looked at it was this: My job was to represent the president. I could not do my job by ignoring more than half the people.

My wife and I had been the guests of Mrs. Graham, the publisher of *The Washington Post,* at her vacation home on Martha's Vineyard. In the summer of 1985, I suggested that she ought to invite Nancy sometime. I had to assure Kay that I wasn't joking.

So it was arranged, and Nancy had the time of her life. I had advised Kay not to invite a bunch of Republicans Nancy already knew, but to invite people she wouldn't otherwise meet.

Kay outdid herself. The guest list included Jackie Onassis, as well as Meg Greenfield, the respected *Newsweek* editor and columnist.

Early on, when Nancy was going through the severest of her Washington criticism, Jackie Onassis had called to offer her encouragement. She said she had been through it, and advised Nancy not to read the papers because it would pass.

They did not become soul sisters, but Nancy was touched that the former Mrs. Kennedy would call. She had always respected and liked her, once was in awe of her, and welcomed the chance to see her under quiet circumstances at the Vineyard. At one point, Jackie said, referring to the press sniping, "You're going to be there [the White House] a long time; you might as well get used to it."

They did not get a chance to exchange more than a few words that night. But it was interesting to me to see how people circled them in separate orbits. Many of them knew Jackie, who had a home there. They were new to Nancy.

Her respect for John Kennedy's widow has not lessened, but I think the awe is gone, a reflection more of Nancy Reagan's new public confidence than anything else. Jackie is even more of a private person.

There must be an unofficial First Families' club out there. At various times, Nancy received other calls of support from Pat Nixon and Margaret Daniel. After JFK's death, Jackie withdrew even more from the public eye. Today I don't think Nancy Reagan would, given a similar fate.

I doubt that more than a handful of people have seen the funny side of Jackie Onassis. She is another flirt, and world-class charmer. I had brought with me a five-pound box of See's chocolates, and after dinner Jackie and I were the only ones attacking this box. This was after I had gone on a crash diet at the White House and shed some forty or fifty pounds.

She said to me, in her whispery voice, "How can you eat this candy and stay so thin? You are so svelte. You're like a young Fred Astaire."

I just melted. Carolyn could hardly stand to have me in the house for a week. After the other guests had gone, we sat around with Nancy, Kay, and Meg Greenfield, rehashing the party, and I could not resist quoting Jackie's compliment. To my dismay, Kay Graham doubted me: "Oh, she said no such thing. I didn't hear it."

But her butler was standing behind me with a coffee service, and he volunteered his support: "Yes, Mrs. Graham, those were her exact words."

Others in and around the White House sometimes resented my bipartisan social contacts, but Nancy always wanted to know what the people were like, and what was said. She was the little girl with her nose pressed up against the candy-store window.

On another trip to Martha's Vineyard, Carolyn and I had lunch with Lillian Hellman, Joe Alsop, Loch Phillips, of the Phillips Gallery, and his wife, Jennifer. Hellman arrived at one o'clock with a tumbler of gin. It was six months before her death, she was nearly blind, and I remember putting a cigarette in her mouth and lighting it for her.

That same day we went for dinner to the home of William Styron, the author of *Sophie's Choice,* and six couples walked out when they saw me. It was their way of protesting the Reagan policies, I imagine. Those who stayed laughed about it. I didn't

know any of the ones who left, and if they had been worth
knowing they probably would have stayed.

But it was another lesson in the Washington survival course.
No political party has a monopoly on bad manners or bad taste.

One guest, a novelist, confided that he had a tiny shack behind his house where he does his writing every night. He
claimed he could not write if he was sober, so he drank until
eleven or twelve o'clock and then wrote through the night. I saw
him several months later and he had stopped drinking. He
looked miserable. "I can't write anymore," he complained.

Another guest was Trevanian, the author who goes by only
one name, and whose most popular novel was *Shibumi*. He confided that his weakness was nicotine. "I smoke six packs of ciga-
rettes a day," he told me. "Some nights I sit there in front of a
typewriter four or five hours, just smoking, without hitting a
key. I do it night after night, until the inspiration comes."

Sometimes I think we need more artistic people in government service. They are often eccentric, but their virtue is that,
unlike generals, they want to blow up only themselves.

Nancy Reagan is not uncomfortable among free spirits and
intellectuals. Most people would be surprised by how bright she
is. For all the speculation about her White House role, Nancy
took care to pick her spots. But once into an issue, she was like
a dog with a bone. She just didn't give up. It was Nancy who
pushed everybody on the Geneva summit. She felt strongly that
it was not only in the interest of world peace but the correct
move politically. She would buttonhole George Shultz, Bud
McFarlane, and others, to be sure that they were moving toward
that goal.

The death of someone close causes most of us to look inside
ourselves. It is natural then to think about goals achieved or
abandoned. After Loyal Davis died two years ago, Nancy told
me what a shattering experience it had been. She sat there holding his hand for almost an hour after he was dead. She could not
let go.

We all dread dwelling on morbid matters. But her father's

death so moved her, I finally decided I needed to ask if she had thought about where she and the president would be buried. The question had to be dealt with, since one of the options was Arlington National Cemetery.

When I mentioned it, Nancy said, sharply, "Never." But she realized it was necessary to consider this matter and asked me to recommend some potential sites.

I am not sure even now what my feelings were as we discussed these things. Death, after all, is a part of living. What stayed with me, I guess, was the matter-of-fact way Nancy discussed this with her husband, and how easily they entrusted this most intimate of decisions to my recommendation.

Potomac Fever

*When Carolyn and I flew east for the week of inaugural fes-
tivities, we left our son and daughter in California with their
grandparents.*

*In mid-January, Amanda, then twelve, and Blair, five, flew
across the country by themselves. We had the pleasure of picking
them up at Dulles Airport with a car and driver, a luxury they
had never before enjoyed. We took them on a tour of Washington
at night, past the spotlighted Capitol and the ghostly marble
monuments.*

*It was after eleven o'clock before we had everyone unpacked
and settled down in our new home. I was tucking Blair into bed
when he said, "Dad, can I ask you something?"*

"Sure."

"Is Washington part of the Planet Earth?"

*I held back a laugh and told him, quite honestly, "I don't know
yet, Blair."*

6
Three on
a
Swing

Hugh Sidey, of *Time,* said we sounded like an infield in the American League: Meese, Baker, and Deaver. There was really not much new in the way we were organized or how we represented the president.

Every chief executive since Lincoln has been served by two or more close assistants. Roosevelt had Jim Farley and Tom Corcoran. Kennedy had his brother Bobby and the Irish Mafia. Nixon depended on the Berlin Wall, Haldeman and Ehrlichman.

Perhaps it was the fact that there were three of us that so intrigued the press, or the way we so clearly drew our lines, or that the system worked at all. It did indeed work, which had as much to do with the personality of Ronald Reagan as anything else. If the power we had seemed to others to be more than was healthy—or even more than we actually had—that, too, reflected the Reagan mystique.

I remember the last scene in the movie *The Candidate,* when the room begins to be flooded with people, and the newly elected senator, played by Robert Redford, looks over their heads to his campaign manager, and his lips form the words that the noise drowns out:

"What do we do now?"

In a sense, no candidate can really confront that question in a hard-nosed way until he actually has been elected. For the Reagan team, the question began to nag at us ten days before the 1980 election, while Ronald Reagan and I, the two of us alone, were having a drink on the terrace of his rented farmhouse in Middleburg.

He asked, "What do you think about Dick Allen as a national security adviser?"

I said, "Before you think about that you need to think about a chief of staff."

The thought seemed to surprise him. "Well, I've always assumed Ed Meese would fill that."

I nodded. "Ed may be more valuable in another role. As chief of staff, you need to think about someone who knows Washington, knows the way the town works. We're about to embark on something, Governor, that we don't know a lot about."

He asked if I had anyone in mind.

I said, "Yes, Jim Baker."

That was all. I did not try to sell him, or review his credentials.

Reagan cocked his head. "Jim Baker," he repeated. "That's an interesting thought."

Later that day, I placed a phone call to William Clark in California. I told him I wanted to head off an internal problem before one could develop. Reagan was beginning to get pressure from his closest backers on who should be on his staff. I said I thought he would best be served by someone like Jim Baker, who knew Congress and knew the city and, as the saying goes, had no petitions out with anyone. The key to the puzzle, however, was what to do with Ed Meese.

Clark said, "That's easy. You make Meese chief counsel to the president."

I went back to Reagan with Clark's suggestion, and he saw quickly that it made sense.

There had been a lot of maneuvering going on the past few weeks among those who expected to be part of the new government. During our last stop in Pacific Palisades, Meese had asked me to join him for breakfast. The meeting was a tense one.

Meese was ready for me with one of his famous organizational charts, featuring himself as chief of staff. In it, I had the box that included schedule, press, politics. He wanted my reaction and I withheld it. "Ed, I think we ought to get through the election first," I said.

A few days later, I met with Dick Wirthlin, the campaign pollster and one of its strategists. He confided in me that he had been selected to the White House staff and would be responsible for communications and political operations. Those titles sounded familiar. They had been penciled in on the chart under "Deaver." I asked Wirthlin where he had gotten his information. He said from Ed Meese.

Once again, I had the feeling of a fellow who saw his duty and knew he would catch hell for it. I was going to be putting myself in the middle, trying to do what I thought best for the president-to-be, and still remain fair to a friend. I knew Reagan had tough calls ahead of him.

The day after the election, Meese called and said we ought to meet with the president-elect to set up the staff. Knowing what was coming, I wanted to duck it, and I suggested Meese see Reagan on his own. But the three of us met for lunch and Meese pulled out his organization chart.

The president glanced at it and said, "Ed, I have really thought about this a lot, and I have decided to divide the White House responsibilities. I plan to make Jim Baker the chief of staff and you my chief counsel. Jim will run the White House and deal with legislation. You will have the policy shop."

Meese was hurt and not fully able to conceal it. He devoted most of his public life to Ronald Reagan and never really understood his strengths and weaknesses. Walking out of the house, he turned to me and asked, "Did you know about this?"

I said, "Ed, I really think this is the best thing for everyone, and you ought to sit down with Jim Baker and work it out."

And so they did. The next day, the three of them—Meese, Baker, and the president—met in a room at the Century Plaza Hotel. This time Baker had brought the paperwork: an agreement for the president to sign, spelling out exactly what the roles would be.

For all the references, some flattering, some not, the occasional infighting and the so-called backstage stress, we made it work. I would end up managing Reagan's personal and political needs, and acting when needed as an honest broker between Baker and Meese.

In time, I think we came to enjoy the idea of the Troika, or the Three-Headed Monster. We were a good staff, proof of which was the almost solid front we enjoyed for four years, and the success of Reagan's first term.

The chemistry, to say the least, was interesting.

My support for Jim Baker was as objective as such things can get in Washington. We had been on opposite sides, and hardly knew each other socially. In fact, I had never heard of him until the presidential campaign in 1976. One of Ford's junior staffers had complained that Reagan had not been helping the ticket. The governor read this comment while he was on the road, stumping for Ford in Salt Lake City.

I saw him walk into the lobby of our motel and he was livid. "I am mad as hell," he said. "I have always supported the party, and here I am busting my neck for Ford and I have to put up with this nonsense. Mike, get me Baker on the phone."

We went to our rooms and I put a call through to Howard Baker, the senator from Tennessee. When I handed the receiver to Reagan, he started in on his grievances and didn't stop until, finally, Baker said, "Ron, I agree with you completely, but I don't know what you expect me to do about it."

Reagan was stopped cold. "Oh, hell, Howard, Mike gave me the wrong Baker. I wanted Jim."

For the next four and a half years, whenever I sided with Jim Baker, I heard the same criticism, usually from hard-core conservatives: Deaver would not let Reagan be Reagan; he was— the severest name they could call me—a "pragmatist."

It was also said that I turned against my old friends and went with this patrician Yalie, Baker, who was the kind of person I always wanted to be. There was some truth in that.

Baker kept urging me to attend the Cabinet meetings, to take a stronger interest in the issues. They kept a chair reserved for me and it was vacant 90 percent of the time. I did not see this as my reason for being in the White House, to be bored unconscious at Cabinet meetings. When I did attend one, I had the feeling I was the only person in the room who did not have to worry about a power base. The side door of my office opened on to the ultimate power base: the desk of Ronald Reagan.

The few Cabinet meetings I did attend, or at which I at least stayed long enough to make the roll call, came back to haunt me. What I was supposed to have heard or said there figured in the conflict of interest charges filed after I had gone into business for myself.

My working relationship with Jim Baker was the best I ever had. He was smart and quick, understood better than most how Washington ticked, and assembled good people around him.

I have enjoyed the friendship that grew out of our shared years with the president. Baker is the kind of person who would be attractive to the Reagans. One of his strongest qualities is his refusal to let a problem fester. If he has a difference of opinion with you, he will be right there, in your office, getting it out. He was absolutely tenacious, at times to the point of driving me nearly bonkers. Jim would call ten or twelve times in a morning, checking to be sure I had done something he had mentioned at breakfast.

Baker is one individual I could fully support for any office he sought, possibly because he doesn't want one. He ran for attorney general once, in Texas, and told me many times he would not trade the experience for anything, nor would he go through it again.

Jim is one of the new breed of political managers, as far as one can get from the old backroom boss with the cigar and the derby. He is reserved, handsome, well tailored, a fourth-generation attorney whose great-grandfather had founded one of Houston's most distinguished law firms.

Once a Tory Democrat, he didn't turn Republican until 1970, when he did so to run the Senate campaign of his pal George Bush. I remember when the two of them stopped off to see Reagan in 1978 and advise him that Bush planned to run for president. It was a courtesy that impressed me.

Candor and gentle persuasion are the fish Baker peddles. When the rumor circulated, as it periodically did, that some jockeying for position was going on within the Troika, Baker silenced it: "There is no power struggle going on, as far as I am aware of. I'm not that dumb, because I would lose any power struggle with any of the three Californians who have been with the president for fifteen years."

He referred, of course, to Bill Clark, who had replaced Dick Allen as national security adviser in 1982, Meese, and myself.

Baker was forty when his first wife, Mary Stuart, died of cancer in 1970, leaving him with four young sons to raise. Bush practically pushed him into politics as a way of dealing with the void left by the loss of his wife.

By 1975 he had joined the Ford administration as the undersecretary of commerce, and had married Susan Winston, a friend of his first wife and one of the great ladies I have known.

Baker is an asset to any political leader because he doesn't need the job and he is secure enough to say no. He turned down the national chairmanship after the Republicans lost the White House in 1976. It was Baker who argued in favor of Reagan's debating John Anderson, the articulate, white-haired Republican congressman who ran for president as an independent, and later Carter, even though some on the team had reservations.

Baker never took such positions on a whim. He is probably the most careful individual I have ever met, and a nice balance to my sometimes impulsive nature. If Jim was going on *Meet the Press,* he would have his staff in his office for hours, prepping him.

Where I might go with my instinct, and make a decision off the top of my head, Baker would come around hours later, after giving it a second and third look, and say, "Mike, I don't think you want to do this."

The ceaseless sniping from the far right took its toll on Baker, more than it did on me. I was fairly insulated, after all, by my years as a Reagan loyalist. When a graceful way out of the White House presented itself—trading places with Don Regan—Jim leaped at it.

What no one disclosed at the time was how close Baker came

to making another choice, one that would have surely rewritten the history of Ronald Reagan's second term. Baker was drained and wanted out, wanted a role that would involve him more in the international scene.

When Bill Clark announced he was returning to California, his decision created an opening at the National Security Council, one almost custom-made for the Texan with the tough hide and quiet charm. The NSC had been established under Eisenhower, as a kind of filtering device, to coordinate the various security bodies.

Gradually, the NSC evolved into such a huge bureaucracy that the head of the council became what he was not designed to be: the principal adviser on foreign policy to the president. The predictable outcome was a clash with the secretary of state, a conflict only Henry Kissinger avoided—by assuming both roles.

Dick Allen and Bill Clark believed they spoke for the president on foreign affairs, and saw it as their charge to align the State Department with whatever they believed that policy to be.

Allen never fully accepted the existence of a new China policy. He was actively pro-Taiwan and, in fact, had represented Taiwanese clients before he joined the White House. Clark's obsession was the Soviet Union. He saw no hope in any policy that relied on trusting the Russians, argued against any attempt to improve that relationship, and did what he could to slow it down.

He felt betrayed—by Mike Deaver—when Nancy and I were able to persuade the president to tone down the "Evil Empire" language Clark had favored. When Bill went to Nancy, and was told point-blank that I stood with her, he decided it was time to go home.

Jim Baker agreed to take the job of national security adviser on one condition: that I succeed him as chief of the White House staff. I had prepared myself to leave, and was eager to get on with a career in business. Baker knew just how much arm to twist: "I'll be right downstairs. We'll have the same team and it will be good for the president."

He meant it literally: "downstairs." The NSC offices were in the White House basement. He was right, of course; it would

have been good for the president, and almost assuredly there
would have been no arms sold to Iran, no Swiss bank accounts
or secret funds diverted to the Contras, no foreign policy seem-
ingly created by Rube Goldberg.

A press release was written and the president had the changes
on his desk: Baker to the NSC, Deaver as chief of staff. Only
one thing went wrong. Ronald Reagan confided in Bill Clark
and Ed Meese that the moves were coming, and their objections
were heated. I do not think there was much in this that was
personal; they felt as protective of Reagan, in their way, as I
did. Their way was to worry about how the changes would play
on the far right.

Having tried not to malign the motives of Clark and Meese, in
a tiny corner of my heart I believe Baker's reassignment was
blocked only because it was tied to mine. I was disappointed
that the president had let himself be talked out of the decision at
the last moment, and a week or two later I mentioned how I felt
to Nancy.

She seemed surprised. "Mike," she said, "what you have to
understand is that Ronnie wants you to be chief of staff . . .
someday."

So the plan was scrapped, and the NSC position went to Rob-
ert "Bud" McFarlane, who brought with him Admiral John
Poindexter and a marine lieutenant colonel named Oliver
North. For the time being, Baker and I stayed where we were.

The Treasury swap originated with Baker, but he found a willing buyer in Don Regan. Although a Cabinet rank, in the normal order of things, would be viewed as more desirable than
control of the White House staff, Don Regan was intrigued by
the switch. As a former marine colonel and Wall Street star, he
fancied the view from the boss's elbow.

In his first days on the job, he described himself as "the small
end of the funnel" that fed information to the president. The
power that had been shared by three now was held by one, and
the word spread. Don Regan was tightening the White House
operation. He would stop or reduce the leaks, put the press in
its place, instill more efficiency. The early reports were glowing.
No hint of an accident waiting to happen.

"It's an ear job, not an eye job," said Regan, meaning that the mastery of it depended on whose voices were heard. In retrospect, the president would have benefited if so many eyes had not winked or remained closed.

In the meantime, the closeness I once had with Edwin Meese became what I viewed as a casualty of doing business in Washington. I doubt that we will ever get it back, but my admiration for him has not lessened. I had been working under Meese for two years in the governor's office after he succeeded Bill Clark as Reagan's executive secretary. Clark's job was one I thought I might inherit; the ironic reverse of the situation we would face in 1980. But Meese called, and told me he had agreed to take the job with Reagan only on the condition that I stay on as the Number Two man. And I did.

I think I know Ed Meese as well as anyone, and I know him as a decent and considerate man, whose weakness is a tendency to get overconfident—in himself or his abilities, which are multiple. In some ways it boils down to a matter of trust. Meese, a prosecutor at heart, is not by nature a trusting person. But he is an unselfish one.

He comes from a long line of public servants, a father and grandfather who held the office of treasurer of Alameda County. I don't think he has known or wanted any other life. When he leaves the government, I doubt that he will feel an urge to go out and make big money. He will probably teach law somewhere.

In the White House, Meese was, of all of us, including Reagan, the one who fought the hardest for purity in matters of conservative ideology. Many a time I teamed up with Baker because the stubbornness of Meese left no other way. He saw it as disloyalty on my part.

But I was not there to enforce a philosophy. I had one criterion: Was it in the best interest of the president? I did not confuse Ronald Reagan with America, but I often felt what was good for one had to be good for the other.

Meese was a big target for the press and he never handled it well. Through the hearings for his appointment as attorney general, the charges of sweetheart loans and concerns that his political views were extremist, he carried his pain with him. He has a wry sense of humor, but he was unable to use it to deflect the criticisms.

When I encountered troubles of my own after opening my public-relations office, I could still laugh at some of the jabs, such as a *Doonesbury* strip that showed Reagan, at his desk, musing about how nice it had been to visit with Mike Deaver. "What's Mike doing now?" he asks an aide. "He's in aluminum siding" was the reply.

The final panel showed the White House exterior refinished in aluminum siding.

The White House toughened Meese, but I have to say he went through ordeals, personal as well as professional, I don't know that I could have survived. Meese was in San Francisco on a political errand the dreadful night when their son suffered a fatal accident. I took the call from Bobby DeProspero, the head of the Secret Service, who said: "Mike, Scott Meese has been killed in a motor accident. Around midnight or one in the morning. I'm at the hospital and we don't know where to find the Meeses. We're keeping it quiet until you can find them."

I learned where Meese was staying and asked Lyn Nofziger to tell him in person rather than deliver the news by phone. The next time I saw Nofziger his face was still grim. "Don't ever ask me to do that again with anybody, ever, ever," he said.

Whatever he went through, Meese carried out any job he ever undertook, and was simply incapable of quitting. For any or all of our later differences, I have a tremendous respect for both Ed and Ursula.

Of course, it was pointless trying to give Meese advice regarding the media. He refused to play the Washington game, could not or would not take the press into his confidence, and would, as a matter of loyalty or conviction, sit there and deny something he knew to be true.

Baker looks like someone who has just stepped out of *Gentlemen's Quarterly,* but Meese's pudgy shape and face give him no advantage at all. He does not come across as the tough lawman he is, or the affable friend he can be. He just doesn't come across as the fully dimensional person he is.

Meese had one thing in common with Baker. He went to Yale, and from there launched his career in law enforcement. He was a high-profile district attorney in Alameda County, and a lobbyist for the state association of D.A.s. Through that connection he met Ronald Reagan, and joined his staff in 1967 as a secretary for legal affairs.

He grew in the job, and Reagan, with his own strong revulsion for public disturbances, came to respect Meese's judgment in dealing with the violence then spreading across college campuses. Best of all, his private opinions coincided squarely with the governor's in nearly every other area.

Both men have been described as amiable loners, friendly to all but intimate friends to very few.

For my own job description, I am going to hide behind an article that appeared in *Esquire* magazine, written by Laurence Barrett:

"Images, images. Deaver's own image was fuzzy to the outside world. During the administration's first two years, Meese and Baker appeared frequently on television talk shows. They gave speeches . . . and conducted on-the-record press briefings. Deaver did none of that. He was an expert in no objective discipline—not economics, not foreign policy, not administration, not legal affairs, not national political organization. He rarely immersed himself in any one issue unless a serious problem threatened the Reagans. There lay his expertise: How the Reagans thought, felt, reacted. In difficult situations, his habit was to operate inside. . . ."

Of the three of us, only Baker really sailed through without taking his lumps from the press and public. It was Meese who decided not to wake the president at eleven o'clock at night after learning that American fighter jets had shot down two Libyan planes over the Gulf of Sidra.

And Meese, in reaction to the flow of news leaks to the media, kept pushing until the president signed an order that would authorize lie-detector tests for all federal employees. Baker and I helped persuade him to rescind it. "Mr. President," said

Baker, in one of his most telling arguments, "if you think Mike Deaver has never leaked a story, you're in a dream world."

That scene, described in detail elsewhere on these pages, was partly a test of wills. I knew how Meese had worked on Reagan. The president has a weakness for any argument that seems to support law and order. This case was not so simple (they rarely are). To begin with, by requiring such tests, the White House would be colliding with a document called the Constitution. The Fifth Amendment protects our citizens from self-incrimination. Nearly as alarming would have been the suggestion that Reagan had missed an Orwellian danger: the polygraph as an instrument of the government. You don't build a just society on the mistrust of four thousand employees, including your immediate staff.

In truth, we three had access for a critical chunk of time to what one might describe as the home office of the American dream. And then came the day in late May 1985 when we went our separate ways.

I had made my decision to go into private business. Don Regan wanted to move into the White House, and Baker wanted out, and they agreed to swap jobs, Baker becoming secretary of the treasury. It fell upon me to inform the president of the plan and gain his approval.

The president did not require a hard sell. He knew that Baker had given him a three-year commitment, and it had already stretched past four. Jim was itching to take on something else. He had even flirted with the baseball commissioner's job, before it was offered to Peter Ueberroth.

Regan was considerate enough to call and tell me he would not seek Baker's spot if I wanted it for myself. I assured him I was as ready as Jim to find a new challenge.

I was still at my post when the switch was made. I remember the first day I walked Don Regan into the Oval Office as the new chief of staff. "Mr. President," I joked, "I finally brought you someone your own age to play with."

Regan's style was the opposite of Baker's. Regan was his own man, and expected people to be courteous and even deferential. Baker was a great delegator. His staff would tell him he was nuts or blow up at him in meetings, and he would tolerate it. He had no problem with their form of communication.

I might add, as modestly as I can, that in our four-plus years as a team, I was generally the bearer of bad news. The president's distaste for an unpleasant scene has been well documented. And both Baker and Meese were reluctant to turn down other associates, or tell someone his or her services were no longer required. In short, I was the guy who wielded the ax, and I can tell you that is a guaranteed way to develop a flock of ill-wishers.

But I believed in getting rid of a problem as quickly as I could. And I took that position in the cases of Dick Allen, David Stockman, Al Haig, and James Watt. Let me clarify my role. I would find it as hard as anyone else to fire somebody who worked for me. But I could do it for someone else, if doing so served Ronald Reagan.

Jim Baker tried his hardest to involve me more deeply in the substance of the ongoing problems we faced. It embarrasses me not at all to say he failed almost totally. When the policy talk and the breaking down of details dragged on, I could leave a meeting in mid-sentence and catch some air.

I simply have never had much confidence in myself on issues, a situation probably dating back to my college days at San Jose State, majoring in political science, after a brief stab at journalism. Or maybe it is a throwback to my short career as a salesman for IBM. Whatever the reason, I could never sell a car or a vacuum cleaner, but a concept, an idea, these excite me. Here is where I find the challenge.

Only when I thought the president was being poorly advised would I plunge myself into a debate. One summer, Al Haig was pushing one of our planning groups to endorse a move toward global negotiations. What it boiled down to was taking a ton of money from the rich countries and letting the poor and developing nations spend it any way they wanted.

I sat there and listened to this and finally said, "This is ludicrous. You have the most conservative president in this century, and you are trying to get him to adopt the most liberal international position anyone could have."

Haig exploded. "It's easy enough for you young guys"—what a charmer, that Haig—"to sit around this table and philosophize, but the rest of us have to live in the real world."

I said, "I don't know about that, Al. What I do know is that this proposal is not consistent with Ronald Reagan's philosophy."

Wherever Meese and Baker and I disagreed, we dealt with the questions in as reasonable and gentlemanly a manner as we could. A case in point arose in May 1982, at our ritual 7:30 breakfast in Baker's office. I had received a telegram from Benjamin Hooks, the head of the NAACP, who was distressed over an affirmative-action court case that started in New York City and was now making its way on appeal through the federal court system.

The Justice Department was on record as being against this kind of case, in opposition to the NAACP position. Meese made it fairly clear that such a policy would favor intervention by Justice. "We campaigned on it," he said.

I could see the dismay in Baker's eyes. We were both uneasy, feeling that the White House would appear once again to be unsympathetic to blacks and Hispanics. Baker and I convinced Meese that a closer look was needed. We met again a few days later and went over the same ground. By the third meeting, we had agreed on our recommendation to the president: Justice was to stay out.

So there we were in the Rose Garden, the three of us, with champagne flowing and a nice display of sentiment from the man we had each served in triumph, and occasionally in times tragic or comic.

The Garden party was really my farewell. But it was a chance for a fine group portrait. Baker got a big laugh by giving me the traditional White House kiss-off: "And, remember, Mike, don't call us, we'll call you."

The president promised not to raise "golf balls" in anyone's throat, but he did. Nancy kept her eyes down. And it was one of those rare moments when no one had anything unkind to say.

Later, each of us was asked what made the Troika work. Meese said it was "loyalty to the president that made things go." Baker said, simply, "It's a people business," the implication being that these were good people.

The Speechmaker

If they kept records on this sort of thing, the way they do in baseball, it would be interesting to see where Ronald Reagan ranked among speech givers, in a career or season.

I personally have heard him give seven hundred or eight hundred speeches to audiences of all size and status. I would not say, as I have heard it said of other politicians, that I heard him make the same speech seven hundred or eight hundred times.

Although much has been made of his use of a TelePrompTer in his addresses on national television, I believe Reagan was at his best when he spoke extemporaneously, and often without notes. The only problem would be related to what he called his get-off line, a product of his personality.

He would be driven nearly to a filibuster some nights, trying to think of a clever or touching punch line to end his talk. I would be sitting out in the limo, perhaps with his secretary, Nancy Reynolds, and we would both be wearily checking our watches. When he at last climbed into the car, Reynolds would confront him: "Do you realize you talked for fifty-five minutes?"

He would act genuinely surprised. "Was it that long? Well, those people paid a lot of money for that dinner. I don't think it would be fair to just give them a twenty-minute shot and duck out."

In the period between his last term as governor of California and his first as president, my office in Los Angeles booked his banquet appearances. His fees ranged from $5,000 up to $15,000 and the sponsors were usually large corporations. Once, a charitable group in a small town in Iowa had invited him to speak, and we arrived in the midst of a blizzard.

That kept the crowd down, and one of the directors—a Democrat—complained bitterly that Reagan would accept a fee from a charity. When the comments reached him, along with the news that the dinner would lose money, he sat down and wrote out his personal check to repay the amount of the fee, which meant that he wound up flying across the country and speaking for free.

7
Washington Merry-go-round

There is a temptation on the part of anyone who has been in public life to strike back at the press, to lash out at the unfairness of the advantage it has over each of us. And sooner or later, no matter how open you think you have been, or how friendly the relationship, the press will do a job on you. Not always a big job. Maybe a small job. But it will get you. It is the nature of the business, and what you discover is that you help your cause not at all by cursing, crying, threatening to sue, or simply falling on the floor and stamping your tiny feet.

As an old wise man once said, you never pick a fight with someone who buys ink by the barrel. The free exchange of information is part of what the American political system is about, and in that spirit, I ought to acknowledge my debt to the press. I am much wiser now than when I came to Washington in 1980. And let there be no mistake: I have seen the other side, as well, the discreet and not so discreet use of the press. A trial balloon here, a news leak there. When the infighting gets truly bitter in any president's White House, the rival factions start planting stories in the same spirit with which the old Russians used to throw each other off the back of their sleds—to slow down the wolves. Sometimes, as Marshall McLuhan said, the medium is the message.

I laugh when I recall how really naïve I was when I carried out my first White House assignments. Early on, I flew to Cancun, a resort on the Gulf of Mexico, with Al Haig, his staff and mine, to prepare for a visit by the president. The back of the plane was occupied by newspeople.

During the flight, Haig drifted back there and spent about an hour. Later, the pool reporter came forward to show him a wire-service story that had been prepared. I heard Haig say, "Those sons of bitches. I didn't say that."

I read the story over his shoulder and said, "They don't quote you. They quote a senior administration source."

Haig said, "That's me."

The fact is, just about whatever I know today about the press and public relations, I learned either from Ronald Reagan or by osmosis. I had a few journalism courses at San Jose State, but I must admit that in terms of residual value, I feel the way Joe Namath did when a sportswriter once asked him if he majored in basket weaving at Alabama.

"No," replied Namath. "Basket weaving was too tough, so they put me in journalism."

I was never entirely comfortable with being known as the man in charge of Ronald Reagan's personality. Two things are crucial to surviving in Washington: 1) You must believe that what you are doing is more important than you and your personal needs; and 2) you must not confuse the image with the reality.

One may not be more essential than the other. But you do need to be able to tell them apart.

Someone once said, on one of those television talk shows, that "Mike Deaver changed the perception of how public relations fits into politics."

I am unsure if that was intended as a compliment. But you have to inspire support for the president if you are going to rally support for his policies. This is basic. This is the essence of good P.R. This is politics.

When the economy started to pick up toward the end of 1980, we were searching for any development that we could showcase to reflect a good trend. A staffer walked into my office one day and said housing starts were up for the first time in five years and we ought to get the president down to the press room to make an announcement.

At such moments, you go with your instinct. This was mine: "No, find me a city with the most dramatic increase in housing starts in America. And get it back to me fast."

The city turned out to be Fort Worth, Texas. I had the president fly to Fort Worth, and he made the announcement at a housing development there, surrounded by a bunch of construction workers in hard hats.

You get only forty to eighty seconds on any given night on the network news, and unless you can find a visual that explains your message you can't make it stick.

VISUALS. I am sure the purists, who want their news unfiltered and their heroes unrehearsed, gag on the word *visuals*. But in the Television Age, it hasn't happened, or at least it hasn't really registered, if people can't see what you see.

When we were going to make an announcement about the placing of a major order for the B-1 bomber, in the early stages of the 1984 campaign, some people close to the president were paranoid over the prospect that Walter Mondale might use this to raise the war and peace issue. But the B-1 bomber had another potential: It meant forty thousand jobs in California.

So the decision was made. I wanted the president to be photographed standing next to a B-1 bomber, and I wanted a sign so big that you could barely see the aircraft. The sign said: PREPARED FOR PEACE. My standing joke with Bill Hinkle, the head of the advance team, was: If you can't give me a good visual, give me a big sign.

I looked on this area as the creative side of my work. I do not mean to suggest that the feeling was comparable to, say, Busby Berkeley choreographing two hundred dancers in a musical comedy. But when you stood at a distance and surveyed the Normandy coast, or the Demilitarized Zone between North and South Korea, you had the sense of sweep and panorama that any director must feel.

And it is in this kind of environment that Ronald Reagan did more than star. He glowed.

*   *   *

I have never seen the president get emotional or weep over anything related to him in a personal way, whether a family loss or a disappointment or failure of his own. I am told he broke down during his eulogy for the actor Robert Taylor, but that was one of those times where, as he says, he will puddle up. He also grew misty-eyed when he spoke on the valor of the soldiers on the Normandy beaches, the glories of yesteryear.

But the scene that touched me the most had no audience to speak of, no big or dramatic backdrop. Reagan was to have a private meeting with the Polish ambassador, who had defected. The ambassador and his wife were ushered into the Oval Office, and the two men sat next to one another in plush-leather wing-back chairs. Vice-President Bush, and the ambassador's wife, sat facing them on a couch.

The ambassador had in his hand a pocket-sized note pad with the wire rings and lined paper, and he was obviously referring to notes he wanted to give to the president of the United States. Meanwhile, his wife, a tiny, delicate-looking woman, kept her head in her hands the entire time, while George Bush put an arm around her shoulders to comfort her.

The ambassador said, "It is unbelievable to me that I am sitting in the office of the president of the United States. I wish it were under better circumstances."

He begged the president never to discontinue Radio Free Europe. "You have no idea," he said, "what it meant to us to hear the chimes of Big Ben during World War Two. Please, sir, do not ever underestimate how many millions of people still listen to that channel behind the Iron Curtain."

Then, almost sheepishly, he said, "May I ask you a favor, Mr. President? Would you light a candle and put it in the window tonight for the people of Poland?"

And right then, Ronald Reagan got up and went to the second floor, lighted a candle, and put it in the window of the dining room.

Later, in what I still recall as the most human picture of the Reagan presidency, he escorted his guests through the walkway and out to the circular drive on the South Lawn of the White House. In a persistent rain, he escorted them to their car, past the C-9 Secret Service post, holding an umbrella over the head of the wife of the Polish ambassador, as she wept on his shoulder.

It may have been schmaltz to some, but it was pure American schmaltz.

I doubt that any occupant of the White House since Harry Truman has been more humbled by just being there than has Ronald Reagan. Our first summer in Washington, it was hot enough to make most of us repent. There was a ceremony on the South Lawn, and by the time we returned to the Oval Office my shirt was wet enough to cling to my skin. I removed my coat and gave my shirt a few tugs, airing it out. Idly I said, "Mr. President, take your coat off, you'll be more comfortable."

He said, "Oh, no, Mike. I could never take my coat off in this office." He meant it. Other than those occasions when he might return from a radio show in whatever casual clothes he had been wearing—a polo shirt or a flannel shirt—I never saw him shed his coat if he was wearing one in his office.

In its simplest form, my job was to let that man, and those values, come across to the American people. I wanted them to know him as I did. For me to succeed in that respect meant he would have their trust.

His feelings toward the press have changed less than Nancy's, who once held them in somewhat higher esteem. One of her oldest friendships is with Mike Wallace, who started out in radio with Tex McCrary and Jinx Falkenburg, a husband and wife team who were close pals of her mother. Nancy sometimes confided in Frank Reynolds of ABC, and his death from cancer hit her hard.

She was fond of Tom Brokaw, until the NBC anchor wrote a piece for *Rolling Stone,* where he developed at length the theme of Ronald Reagan's shallowness. That was four years ago and she has not forgiven him yet.

She is much more cynical and mistrustful, more wary about all of them, than when she first moved into the White House. The president has understood that many in the working media disagree with his philosophy. He has been known to write long, almost scholarly letters to those who question his positions in a reasonable spirit. A story will upset him if he feels it is unkind or unfair, but not for long. His anger is more likely to focus on the press if information is leaked and printed. Press leaks confuse him; he can't relate to the kind of "internal" scheming or competition that such an act implies. He finds it difficult to believe that anyone who works for him would plant a story that exposes a division in the ranks, or treads on a decision yet to be made.

If a reporter contradicted a statement or one of his anecdotes, he would nearly always feel his words or meaning had been twisted. But this kind of criticism he shrugged off as the nibbling of ducks. Any attack on Nancy was on another level. The speculation about her role behind the scenes of the Iranian scandal, the idea that she was a Svengalian figure, left him sputtering. Anger can be useful to him if it is scripted, if he had time to build up to it. But he tends to be rattled by his own sudden, blind anger.

He told reporters the stories about Nancy trying to run the White House were "contemptible fiction. If I seem angry I am. You've touched a nerve there." That was an answer he gave some thought to. The rumors had offended him, as a husband and as a man who was supposed to be running the country.

The Irangate controversy had less to do with the media than with mistakes in policy. Until then, Ronald Reagan enjoyed the most generous treatment by the press of any president in the postwar era. He knew it, and liked the distinction. Reporters responded to his decency, his bigness: He was comfortable attending a fund raiser for the John F. Kennedy Library, with Ted Kennedy as his host, where Jimmy Carter would not have been.

Most of all, after Johnson, Nixon, and Carter, the press did not want to be accused of destroying another president. When they were tough on him, in those infrequent times over the years, his popularity was able to absorb it.

Whatever was said or written, he rarely saw any of it as something personal. He is entertained by Sam Donaldson, and takes a kind of pride in having helped make him a media star. A diehard Republican asks him, "How can you stand that guy?," and he will reply, "Sam is Sam, that's all."

Nancy Reagan never misses a morning or evening newscast, or any of the Sunday panel shows. The president is a newspaper addict. His regular fare included *The Washington Post, The New York Times, The Wall Street Journal,* and the *New York Post.* I routinely ordered five out-of-state papers, changing the subscriptions each month so he could widen his perspective.

There really is an affliction called Potomac fever. You especially notice it when you get to a city such as San Antonio, Texas. The president, Jim Baker, and I had made a political trip to Texas, and taken a day off for a turkey shoot.

This was at the peak of the Dick Allen problem: The national security adviser was being pressured to resign after his ethics and judgment had been called into question. He had accepted, placed in a safe, and forgotten a cash gift of one thousand dollars a Japanese publisher had intended for Nancy Reagan—unknown to her. Reports of other gifts accepted by Allen had surfaced.

The only newspaper we could find that Sunday was a San Antonio edition. The three of us huddled over it, eager to see how the story was developing. We had to turn to page 18 before we found it.

The office of James Brady and Larry Speakes, of course, had the daily responsibility for the give-and-take with the press. They were the front line. When I dealt directly with reporters, it was largely to provide color or background for their stories. And, at all times, my goal was to put the president in a favorable light. There was no pretense about that, on my part or theirs.

Certainly I leaked a story or two in my time. But never for vindictive reasons, and never information that I knew would have been detrimental to the country or to the White House.

Curiously, in my adherence to these goals, I found myself taking what others often regarded as the moderate, or even liberal, position within the administration. I never knew whether to be flattered or upset. To the extent that I had a political philosophy, it was conventionally conservative. But I was never a fanatic. I never divided people into Us and Them as Pat Buchanan loved to do.

I generally liked reporters, found them interesting, bound by their natures or by tradition to be cynical, but with a certain sporting attitude toward anyone who met them halfway.

It is true that if you forget that their role is so often an adversarial one, you are going to get burned, and your clients with you. It was because of a story I gave to a reporter that an address by Reagan to the British Parliament, at Westminster Hall, was canceled. The British Labour party raised unmitigated hell at the idea of an American political leader invading this historical chamber. When the furor would not subside, the invitation was withdrawn.

The speech would have been the first by a foreign head of state. I saw that news as favorable to the president, and a chance perhaps to repay a courtesy to a reporter who had been helpful. And it cost us.

The reporter I owed a favor to was George Skelton of the *Los Angeles Times*. I had been working in London through the royal palace, and we received word that the queen had approved of the president's appearance. I leaked that story to Skelton, not stopping to realize that neither the prime minister nor Congress had been notified. This would be akin to the White House agreeing to a joint address of Congress by, say, Helmut Kohl of West Germany, not informing the speaker's office, and then having Kohl's itinerary appear in print.

If the right etiquette had been observed, the protests could have been weathered, and the speech would have taken place. My ignorance of the system had blown it, and if I felt any lower I could have tunneled my way back across the Atlantic.

Win some, lose some.

Then there are the days when you have to play what politicians call "hardball." (In baseball, when managers or players are required to do something distasteful, I'm sure they refer to it as "politics.")

On one occasion I was interviewed in Paris by an NBC correspondent who shall remain nameless. Before the camera came on, he said, "Now, I am going to ask you how much this trip is costing the American taxpayers."

I said, "That's fine, as long as you don't mind my responding by asking if NBC knows that you brought your wife along for a two-week tour of Europe at their expense."

He began to sputter. "You wouldn't!"

I said, "Let's turn on the camera, ask your question, and we'll see."

He never asked the question.

The speech that had been scheduled for Westminster Hall was moved to another forum. I felt guilty and embarrassed. But this was one of those times when the image mattered little in the end. What mattered was that Reagan did address both houses of Parliament, and his speech was an eloquent one. I was both proud and grateful. He had taken me off the hook.

The ceremonies I orchestrated in Normandy and on the Korean border may be what most people remember about my White House service. I do not want to make the coverage sound more important than what was represented there. But I will not apologize for being preoccupied with television. There is simply no way to exaggerate the influence of that medium in the political life of this and other nations.

I firmly believe that television has absolutely changed our military strategy, that we will never again fight a major ground war. Americans simply do not want to see mass killings on the TV screen in their living rooms—or wherever they keep their TV sets. You can strafe Libya for thirty minutes, but you can't do it day after day, and you can't send in the troops.

Possibly the only successful ground action this country has taken since World War II was Grenada, or at least we perceive it as such. We got away with it by establishing special ground rules, by not letting the press in and justifying it later. We loved Ernie Pyle and Bill Mauldin, adored seeing the big show on the newsreels twice a month at the neighborhood cinema. *But it was not in our living rooms.* You had to leave home to see it.

It is a strange, enduring, and sometimes symbiotic relationship that Washington has with the press. You need them and they need you. It is not unlike the partnership I once heard of between the performers and a fellow who ran a flea circus out of a box on Forty-second Street in New York. When the act was over—don't ask me what the performers actually did—the owner let the fleas crawl over his arm and enjoy a free meal. It was a fair deal. They lived off each other.

My legacy to the White House may be the so-called "Deaver Rule." I had watched the confusion of the Carter press conferences, and I established at the start this basic principle: the president, alone or with another head of state, would not take questions from reporters who were jumping up and down. They would sit in their chairs and raise their hands, or there would be no press conferences.

I fought my share of battles with the media, individually and collectively, but I hope without meanness or pettiness. At times, fairly large issues were at stake. And I am not certain how the scorecard would reflect the outcome.

I have always believed that among Richard Nixon's Watergate mistakes, one of the most costly was his decision to board up the old swimming pool and create a new press room. In doing so, he moved the media out of the executive offices and into the West Wing—right next door to the Oval Office. So Ronald Reagan, like Carter and Ford and Nixon before him, has to walk right past the press to reach his living quarters.

When the president was shot, his doctors said he needed to get out in the air. There was nowhere he could easily and freely walk except the Rose Garden, which was next to the press room. I finally had to stage a phony press briefing, and get them all out of the way, so that Reagan could spend a few minutes in his garden.

One night, Cap Weinberger and George Shultz were in my office and needed to talk to the president on a matter of national security. It was not something that could be discussed on the phone. Had we walked over to the residence at that hour of the evening, the press would have seen us and suspected something. My office had a back door. So we made our exit, and with a flashlight in my hand, I led the secretaries of defense and state across the South Lawn, sneaking in between bushes and shrubbery to reach the president without being seen.

I may not be on historically secure ground with this thought, but who knows? If Nixon had stayed the hell away from the swimming pool, and not relocated the press, he might never have been forced out of office. If the reporters had not seen quite so much of him, passing by their new press room, they might have liked him better.

It is awkward at times to draw the line between what is irresponsible and what is merely inconvenient. After the wounding of the president, the press kept digging for stories on the new security measures that were instituted. These included our using a dummy limousine and flak teams on rooftops when the president appeared in public, even the fact that Reagan would on occasion wear a bulletproof vest.

All this and more was being given a show-and-tell on the networks. I called in all three bureau chiefs and appealed to their better instincts. I said, "Fellows, I have never asked you to kill a story or to run one. But I am telling you that you are now compromising all the security measures we need to protect the president."

Perhaps the reaction was not as abrupt as it seemed to me at the time. But within minutes, the White House correspondents were on the South Lawn, informing their viewers that Mike Deaver had just told them not to demonstrate how the new security techniques worked—and then proceeding to explain each of them.

A week later I was at a dinner with Bill Paley, the venerable board chairman of CBS. I told him I felt all the networks had made the job of protecting the president more difficult.

"What would you have us do?" he asked.

"To begin with, I believe your people would want to show some respect for the trauma the president, and the country, just went through."

Paley thought I was quibbling, that we were talking about a question of judgment, even news values. "And if it was up to you," he said, "how would you go about seeking this cooperation you seem to feel you need."

I said, "Oh, that wouldn't be hard. I would just have the FCC eliminate ratings for news programs. You claim that news is not the same as entertainment. So why do you need ratings?"

Paley had the look of a man folding his cards. "Well," he said, "that's our big money-maker, the news."

The news media are not quite a fourth branch of government, but they don't miss by much. The industry deserves credit for the role it exercises in ferreting out corruption and wrongdoing. But, obviously, it takes an occasional scattershot approach that finds people guilty by association, or guilty by accusation.

This obsession with the most obscure detail of a public person's past and private life is troubling. It was not so long ago that no one ever saw a photograph of Franklin Roosevelt in a wheelchair. One day, however, Reagan was to be treated at Bethesda Naval Hospital for a bladder infection, and in an off-hand way he told me not to bother including it in the daily press briefing.

When I said we could not ignore it, he demanded to know why. "Because it's minor, and if we don't disclose it they will speculate that it is something far worse, and the next thing you know there will be rumors bouncing around that Reagan has cancer."

He sort of threw up his hands. "What would you have me do" he said, "go down to the press room and unzip my pants?"

All of this intimate medical disclosure began with Dwight Eisenhower's first heart attack, when we learned more than we wanted to know about the cardiovascular and digestive systems. There has been a tendency by the press ever since to demand of our leaders a kind of public strip search. Many found this embarrassing and unnecessary, but Reagan was the first in a long time to overcome it.

Perhaps that was due to his age, or the memory of his shooting, or television and his ability to use it well. In every poll I have seen in the past three years, nearly 70 percent of the American people say they get their news from television. The number alone is scary and ought to cause those who are still literate to sit down and think about the day when we will simply plug the TV cord right into our eye sockets.

As a so-called image maker, I am torn between thinking about how I can best take advantage of this trend, and where it is likely to lead us. It is not hard to picture a scenario not unlike *The Dating Game,* where three candidates give their qualifications, smile, and answer questions about how old they were when they were allowed to car-date, and the studio audience presses a button to indicate their favorite.

For reasons I have not stopped to analyze, but probably related to my having grown up in the last generation not baby-sat by television, I am partial to the print media and the people who work there.

Without question, I regard *The Washington Post* and *The New York Times* as the most influential news organizations in the world—in terms of their impact on the American political structure. I am especially fond of Kay Graham, and take a kind of perverse pleasure in watching her squirm when I say such things as "It must be an awesome responsibility, knowing that you and your publications [the *Post* and *Newsweek*] have the power to elect presidents or throw them out, start wars or end them."

Her usual reflex is to put her hands over her ears and repeat to herself, "No, no, no."

I suppose my all-time personal favorite among newspeople was the late Frank Reynolds of ABC. For the business he was in, Frank had an usually sweet disposition. I always respected his thoroughness, but he won me forever the day the president was shot, and he was handed the bulletin that Jim Brady was dead. When the rumor soon proved to be false, he exploded on camera, in front of millions of viewers, with: "Dammit, check these things out before you hand them to me."

There are certain reporters who develop an aura about them, so that when they say or write something it is automatically picked up by everyone else. Lou Cannon of *The Washington Post* has covered Reagan for twenty-five years, and whatever he writes about him is usually considered gospel. He is not often wrong, and I rate him among the most careful of newsmen.

Another reporter who has my total respect is Hedrick Smith of *The New York Times*. I once asked Smith to hold a story that reflected on our relations with the West German government. That was not a request I made lightly, and up to then I'd had no real success that I can recall. But we were at a touchy moment in our negotiations over the Western Alliance, and the story had the potential to cause real damage. I told him, "You're the only guys who have this story. It happens to be true, but printing it now will be harmful to the national interest. That is as much as I can tell you."

Smith consulted with his editors and they pulled the story, to my surprise—and gratitude.

I have been partial all my life to those who love what they do and work hard at it. I have found that very few people are really happy in their jobs. Helen Thomas is one who is, and she is always running at the front of the pack, wherever the pack is. She must file four or five stories a day and, amazingly, manages to remain fairly objective. When I left the White House, Helen wrote me a letter that meant much to me.

For quite a while, this entire administration ran well ahead of the law of averages in its treatment by the press. Most of us made an effort to be honest and accessible, and when that failed we tried to be civil. One of the recurring criticisms of the Carter administration had been the failure of Carter's personal staff to get out of the bunkers, mingle with the natives, and learn the local customs.

Six months after Carolyn and I had moved into our house, we were invited to dinner at the home of Polly and Clayton Fritchey, whose name is familiar in Washington social circles and in the Democratic party. Fritchey had been Harry Truman's press secretary. All the old cave dwellers were there. We had not yet gotten to know Kay Graham, and at one point she asked me what had surprised me the most since my arrival in Washington.

"The fact that I am sitting here," I said, "and that you and your friends seem to think that I'm someone important."

I wasn't being flippant. I was flattered by their attention and it would be dishonest to deny it.

These were the people who made Washington work—on those occasions when it did work. They lived there, had invested their years and their energy in the city and in the system. Compared to them the rest of us were migrant farmers, picking grapes for four years and moving on to the next stop. They might disagree with you on a wide range of subjects, maybe on all of them, but it did not prevent them from being kind.

I was barely into my second year on the White House staff

when Rowland Evans and Bob Novak flattened me in a column, accusing me of using my position to help former clients of mine in California. The people they mentioned were never my clients. But the attack, the insinuations, left Carolyn in tears. Polly Fritchey knew I was out of town. As soon as she read the article, she called Carolyn and insisted on taking her out to lunch. She spent the afternoon explaining how Washington worked. I am not sure the conversation eased Carolyn's mind a great deal, but at least she came away feeling I wasn't a special case.

The press could ruin your day, the newscasters your night. I anticipate your objection. It is bizarre to let the media invade so much of one's thought, and to alter the daily mood. But it is like trying to ignore a pimple on your nose. You get cross-eyed.

I was fortunate in that I could always walk out of my office, which had been Jimmy Carter's old study, and into the sanctuary of Ronald Reagan. Whatever crisis was around the corner, I could count on him to put things in perspective.

I walked in on him one morning, shortly after the Reagans had entered the service of a new puppy, a huge, shaggy, Belgian cattle dog named Lucky. Frankly, the dog drove me nuts. Keep in mind that I would have been at the White House since six in the morning, with one or two meetings behind me and a full agenda to discuss. And the president would be in the Oval Office, with his dog, trying to teach him obedience.

I would cough and suggest that we really needed to get going. He would pretty much ignore me. "Here, Lucky. Here, Lucky."

Finally, in frustration, on that particular morning, I said, "Mr. President, you need to get that dog out of here. He's going to end up pissing on your desk."

Ronald Reagan looked up and said, "Why not? Everyone else does."

The Protocol

INAUGURATION DAY, 1980:

It is traditional that the president-elect receive the military honors of the four branches of service, their units parading past while he stands on the highest of the White House steps.

There was an army general at his side, and as the troops passed they would do an eyes right and snap off a salute. I heard the president ask, "Is it appropriate for me to return their salute?"

The general replied, rather officiously, I thought: "It is appropriate, sir, if your head is covered."

Hatless, the president nodded and deferred to the general, placing his hand over his heart in the traditional civilian manner. Later, he told me, "I really felt uncomfortable not returning those salutes the men gave me, just standing there, motionless."

I said, "Mr. President, you are the commander in chief now, you can do whatever you want."

I saw his eyes light up. And to this day, he salutes everything that moves. When his helicopter touches down at Andrews Air Force Base, and even the maintenance crews are standing at attention, he presses himself against the window and whips off a salute.

I once asked him how he learned to salute so snappily. He said it was how he had been taught when he was making training films in the air force during the war. "You know what they tell you," he said. "You bring it up like honey and shake it off like [manure]."

The Deavers and the Reagans at leisure

With Alexander Haig

Love is . . .

One of us has never been president.

The hunters (Jim Baker at wheel, Secret Service agent in back)

Back at the ranch

The Tipper and the Gipper

To Mike — give us another chorus!
love Nancy + Ron

Applause for the piano player

With Larry Speakes (to my left), briefing the president

A quick read

Arriving in good humor

Reflections: With Baker

8
Putting
Out
Fires

BEIRUT, 1983

One of President Reagan's favorite, and frequent, stories had to do with the difference between two young brothers, one an optimist, the other a pessimist.

The test of their personalities was how they reacted to a garage filled with horse manure. The pessimist ran out crying. The optimist didn't come out at all. When they opened the door, he was shoveling as fast as he could, explaining: "There must be a pony in here somewhere."

Looking for the pony became the Reagan administration's shorthand for trying to find the bright note in an otherwise gloomy situation. It is remarkable, given the vagaries of fate and the designs of opposing forces we could not possibly control, how often we managed to find one. Much of this, I suspect, had to do with the style and attitudes of the president himself.

In the long run my value to him, in whatever way one measures such things, stemmed not from my loyalty or blind obedience but from my willingness to disagree.

Of all the people around him, save Nancy, I knew him well enough, and had the temperament, to say I thought his position

163

was wrong. I might add that I never did so in public. The Reagan administration, more than most, put a high store on being a team player, and I don't think anyone ever mistook me for anything else.

For me, the absolute low point, the closest I came to quitting on principle, came when we did not react as quickly as I wish we had during the bombings—ours and Israel's—of Beirut, Lebanon.

The American people have a great capacity for forgiving, or forgetting, sometimes both, and since then we have been through a series of terrorist attacks, the taking of more hostages, the escalation of the war in Nicaragua, and a crisis over secret arms sales to Iran.

But Lebanon was a carnage that for a time fit into a category all its own. To trace the background of what took place in October 1983, you could go back several weeks or several years: to 1967, when Israel occupied the West Bank; or to 1976, when Lebanon was torn by civil war and Syria's President Hafez al-Assad sent in his troops. What began then as an Arab peace-keeping force became a permanent occupation.

By 1978, Israel had declared a security strip in the southern part of Lebanon and aligned itself with the Christian militia. Keeping track of the Lebanese factions was a major challenge in itself.

There were splinter groups supporting, or supported by, Iran and Syria. There were the Shi'ites and the Sunni Muslims, the Druze, the Christians, and splinter groups related to each of the others but responsible to none. And, of course, there was the Palestine Liberation Organization, under Yasir Arafat.

Lebanon was always an explosion waiting to happen. I am not going to attempt here a history of the region, or of the violence that took place in the period that reached a horrid climax with the massacre of 241 U.S. marines. In any such analysis, it is mandatory to toss around phrases such as "ancient hatreds" and "sectarian strife."

But the elements that drew the United States into the blood-bath began with what seemed another of those predictable flareups on that turbulent border that joins Israel and Lebanon.

In response to continuing PLO attacks, Ariel Sharon, the Israeli defense minister, sent his tanks rolling across the border in June 1982. Called Operation Galilee, the drive was said to be aimed at securing a buffer zone free of PLO influence twenty-five miles into southern Lebanon.

But against little resistance, Sharon saw an opportunity to drive the PLO entirely out of Lebanon. Israeli warplanes pounded Syrian missile sites in the Bekaa Valley. Its tanks and gunboats shelled the PLO bunkers and hideouts in West Beirut, and while a stunned world marveled at the speed of the operation, Israel suddenly had surrounded Beirut.

Sharon was on the brink of achieving his goal, of all but eliminating the PLO, but the cost was going to be clearly excessive. Arafat's forces were dug in behind civilian lines, mingling with the population, and the PLO leader threatened to take the city down with them. The immediate question was, how far would Israel allow Sharon to go?

Inside the Reagan administration there was bitter division. For weeks I sat there and listened as the National Security Council briefers kept telling Reagan Israel could win, *he* could win, by letting Sharon's tanks and infantry clean out the terrorists once and for all, in the process driving Syria back across its own borders.

Of course, this strategy risked a Mideast nightmare that might have ignited the Third World War. Could we really afford to take that chance? And, I wondered, could we continue to stand by, publicly denounce the Israeli incursion, and privately encourage them even as the civilian casualties mounted?

The NSC is filled with junior military officers. They met with the president daily at 9:30 A.M., and half an hour later they would be gone. On this particular day, I walked back into my office, and sat there, seeing nothing, thinking nothing, for a few minutes or several, I didn't know. For a week the evening newscasts had carried footage of buildings flattened, of bodies without limbs lying twisted in the streets. From my office next door, I could walk in on the president without going through a secretary. I did so now, and said, "Mr. President, I have to leave."

He looked up sharply. "What do you mean?"

I said, "I can't be a part of this anymore, the bombings, the killing of children. It's wrong. And you're the one person on the face of the earth right now who can stop it. All you have to do is tell Begin you want it stopped."

We looked at each other for a long moment. And I think he saw in his own mind the pictures that had so filled me with revulsion. There was just one of those connections, that instant of recognition that says, "My God, what have we done?"

I am uneasy with movie references in matters that have to do with blowing up people in the real world. But in this instance, Ronald Reagan was the central figure, and he of all people would understand. It was the look on the face of the colonel, played by Alec Guinness, in *The Bridge on the River Kwai,* when he realized he had been defending a bridge that would aid his country's enemies.

Reagan rang his secretary and asked her to get Menachem Begin on the phone. In the meantime, George Shultz had joined us and added his endorsement of the president's intervention. When the call came through he told the Israeli prime minister, in the plainest of language, that the shelling had to stop, that Israel was in danger of losing the moral support of the American people. His final words were: "It has gone too far. You must stop it."

Twenty minutes later, Begin called him back and said he had just issued the orders to Ariel Sharon. The bombings had ceased. There were no planes over Beirut. When he hung up the phone, Ronald Reagan looked up and said, seriously, "I didn't know I had that kind of power."

If anything, I am most proud of that moment. Whatever my judgment was worth to him, I felt I had used it to persuade him to follow his own humane instincts. And for a time, all too brief, there was a recess in the madness of Lebanon.

Shortly thereafter a truce was arranged, and the marines went in as part of a multinational force to assure, and to supervise, the safe and orderly withdrawal from Beirut of the remaining PLO guerrillas. They were flown out to other lands, with the main force removed to Tunisia.

Israel had achieved part of its goal, but somehow Arafat had scored a moral victory. He had survived. He, or his supporters, would be heard from again—in the customary, bloody way.

A terrorist bomb then killed Bashir Gemayel, the newly elected president of Lebanon, in September 1982. The marines, who had just finished their escort duty, went back in to buy time while Gemayel's brother, Amin, tried to establish a government. It is too pat, too easy to say now that we should not have sent them back, that we should not have allowed Lebanon to become our problem.

We failed in our efforts, led by George Shultz, to arrange a simultaneous withdrawal of Israeli and Syrian forces. In May 1983, Israel and Lebanon signed a separate truce, which Syria's Assad ignored.

Uneasy and sporadically violent months passed. And then, on a quiet Sunday morning in late October, a truck loaded with dynamite sped past the sentries and crashed into the building at the Beirut Airport that served as the barracks for the 8th Marine Battalion. The structure collapsed in seconds. It took days to dig through the rubble, and the final death toll reached 241 marines, with another 80 wounded. It was our highest one-day loss since January 13, 1968, when 246 American servicemen died throughout Vietnam at the start of the Tet offensive.

In West Beirut, another bomb blew apart a building that housed French paratroopers, killing 58.

When it was all over, when the last of the marines had been evacuated to ships offshore, and our bombs had stopped shelling the Lebanese hillsides when the Israelis had pulled back across their own border, not much had really changed. The Christian militiamen had rampaged through two PLO refugee camps, killing some 300 people, mostly civilian, while Israeli security guards were accused of looking the other way. There was a grave strain, temporarily, on relations between our country and our closest ally in the Mideast. When the final count was made, the Israelis had suffered 3,800 dead and wounded, almost as many casualties as in their triumphant Six Day War of 1967.

The Shi'ites and the Sunni Muslims, the Druze and the Christians and the Syrians went back to killing each other.

What a hellish waste it all had been.

I do not claim that my pleadings led to any kind of a victory. But we helped end the bombing of Beirut. Some lives were saved. Some sense of reason intruded on the killing, at least for a while.

Later, the president and I disagreed on his commitment to the Contras. It was by necessity that I had found myself trying to be a moderating influence on Ronald Reagan. He needed no reinforcement from the right. Months after I had left the White House, I called him and said, "I worked four and a half years to keep the right-wingers from getting you out in front on this Central America issue. Now, Mr. President, for you to go on television to push for more public support of the Contras is a mistake. It is the wrong cause at the wrong time."

He said, "No, no, I have to do it. I believe in it."

I said, "My concern is what it may cost you in the process. You may lose the budget vote, the Jordanian arms vote. And the Russians are likely to say, 'We don't need to talk to this guy anymore.' Now that is what you have at stake."

There was dead silence on the line.

Obviously, I did not dissuade him. I wish I had. He has his arguments in support of the Contras. But I never felt the issue was as clear-cut for the American people: that we were so certain of being on the right side there as to justify putting all our chips on the table. By the spring of 1987, I worried that he was being dragged into a bottomless pit. It is hard for the average American to see Cuba as the all-powerful villain in Central America, when so many of the countries friendly to us in that hemisphere have little sympathy for the Contras. Nor is it easy for the average voter to see why Nicaragua, the Sandinistas, represent a threat to us. I am personally convinced that they do.

There were, of course, differences among all the president's men, on a wide scope of issues, but we tried to resolve them in a gentlemanly way, and to the extent that we could agree on what was best for Ronald Reagan. As for the image or reputation that I acquired, there was this appraisal from Laurence Barrett, one of the senior White House correspondents:

"The drab gray suits and muted ties that Deaver preferred

. . . a professed modesty about his understanding of complicated issues—all this contributed to a stereotype that Deaver was really a glorified servant to the Reagans, with some doubt attending the adjective." (Aside to Barrett: WHAT? You mean I wasn't glorified?)

"But to imagine Deaver's role as primarily that of a political Jeeves would be like describing an elephant merely as an animal with large ears. His rapport with reporters helped to sell Reagan's line of goods. His unerring instinct for situations in which Reagan would come across well brought the President into settings unusual for him—a working class black high school in Chicago, a temporary dike holding back floodwaters in Fort Wayne—and that yielded yet more positive images."

Many of the media, Barrett among them, suspected I was too much like my boss when it came to thinking through the issues. But in the end, you really have only your instincts, all you have been taught and experienced. I always led from my gut when I gave advice. I knew no way to be clever about it. More than the others around the president, I talked from instinct.

My instinct was sound on Jim Baker, wrong on an old friend, Bill Clark.

When charges were made that Dick Allen had accepted gifts, and cash, in arranging interviews for a Japanese publisher with Nancy Reagan, I made the judgment that his future effectiveness would be impaired, and urged the president to move quickly in accepting Allen's resignation.

I never believed that Dick Allen deliberately did anything improper. There was nothing to suggest that he was the kind of fellow who would use his office for personal gain. I think he tossed a watch and a few bills into a safe and forgot about them. We were never close, although Dick was a good friend of my former partner, Peter Hannaford. Our styles really didn't mesh.

It was one of those conflicts the president dreaded and wanted to think that the press had contrived. The day Allen resigned, I was in the hall when the president was going out the door. He stopped and looked at me and said, "This has been a tough day." It was just so hard for him to address that kind of problem.

I thought Clark, because of his close personal ties to Ronald

Reagan (and to me), would be an ideal replacement. It simply did not work out. Clark was a novice in foreign affairs and quickly sided with Ed Meese on issues that found them opposed by Jim Baker. And I generally stood with Baker. Now we had two-on-two, a stalemate. In the end, I think Clark had a different idea of what his role would be in Washington, and he was relieved to get back to California.

The White House staff was split right down the middle between the moderates and the conservatives. Dick Darman, who had worked for Baker, was clearly a pragmatic guy. When Clark suspected Dick of leaking some piece of information, he changed the computer codes on the entry lock to the NSC briefing room, the Situation Room, so Darman could not get in. In retaliation, Darman had a coded entry installed on his office door.

It was during this period of semi-rampant paranoia that I wandered into the Oval Office one morning and found Ronald Reagan and Ed Meese huddling over a document. I pulled up a chair and asked Ed what they were talking about. No answer.

The president said, "Okay, if you guys think this is the right thing to do," and he reached for a pen and signed the document. I asked what he had just signed and he slid the paper across the desk to me. It was the authorization for the attorney general to conduct widespread lie-detector tests.

I wasted no time in getting to Jim Baker, and a short while later we went back to the White House, where the president was having lunch with George Bush and George Shultz. Baker said, "I understand you signed an order authorizing lie-detector tests."

And before the president could reply, George Shultz said, "Well, if you have, you're going to be without a secretary of state, because this one isn't going to stay around if he is required to prove his loyalty with a lie-detector test."

The president was shaken. Within minutes, he called Meese, Bill Clark, and William French Smith and rescinded the order.

It is an article of faith in government that friends come and go, but enemies are forever. I was Alexander Haig's staunchest defender in the Reagan inner circle until the very end of his tour as secretary of state, when two incidents took place.

First, Konstantin Chernenko died and Haig stopped by my office and insisted that the president had to attend the Soviet premier's funeral. I said, "No way. It would come across as phony if the president's first meeting with the Soviets, among forty other heads of state, was at the funeral of a man he had never met."

Haig said, "I am going to take it up with the president."

I said fine. When Haig made his pitch, Ronald Reagan's answer was almost word for word what mine had been.

The next incident involved a young fellow who worked for me, Greg Newell, who wanted an assistant secretary's job, working with such international organizations as UNESCO. I told Greg I would support him if that was what he wanted.

Then Haig called and said he had a problem. He could not accept Greg Newell because he was supporting someone else. I said I understood. Then he said, "I need your signoff [okay] on my guy."

That I could not give him. "I can't do that," I said. "I have given my commitment to Newell and I can't take it back. Look, why don't we send up both names and let the president decide."

Instantly, he thought the fix was in. It absolutely was not. "Sure," he said, "you're right next door and you'll screw me."

I said, "Look, Al, if you feel that way, why don't we both go to the president and explain the problem, at the same time. You can go first."

Haig brought with him an array of lists and charts, a living record of how many times he felt the White House staff had shafted him, all the appointments forced down his throat. As a final, clinching argument, he said, "If I don't get this appointment my credibility will be ruined."

I said, "Al, I could make the same argument, but the question is, will the president's credibility be hurt or helped?"

Haig spun in his chair. "How dare you speak to me like that," he said. "I have served six presidents."

At that point, Ronald Reagan was losing interest. He said, "Let me think about it," and waved us out. Unknown to me, the paperwork approving the promotion of Greg Newell had already crossed his desk. The president didn't even remember seeing it. Later, of course, Haig thought I had knifed him. He was constantly threatening to resign over this confrontation or that, real or imagined.

When he finally pulled out that paper one time too many, and the president accepted, he could not have been more surprised. His feuds within the staff, of course, have become the stuff of legend. He always referred to us as the "guerrillas" in the White House. Baker was his chief target. But I had a friend who owned a gorilla costume, and playing on the word, I borrowed it the week of Jim Baker's fifty-third birthday.

A Cabinet meeting was going on, and I slipped into the gorilla costume, ran along the colonnade area, and burst into the Cabinet room with a sign that said, "Happy Birthday, Jim, from the White House gorillas." The president broke up, but Haig found no humor in it at all.

Reporters milling around in the Rose Garden got a glimpse of what was going on, put it together, and howled with appreciation. But I suppose I can't truly say that Haig and I parted as friends. The last I heard he was running for president. My guess is that doing so is a fine way to keep up the price of his speaking engagements.

Possibly this is the place to offer an impression of some more of the president's men, not necessarily in descending order:

DAVID STOCKMAN—I first met Stockman when he was recommended by Jack Kemp to prep Reagan for the debates in 1976. He had worked for John Anderson, then switched candidates and helped Reagan defeat Anderson in the debates and in the primaries. He was very facile and quick and impressed everyone with his whiz-kid instincts. He had attended divinity school, at least partly to avoid the Vietnam war. Within the Reagan inner circle he would prove himself to be something other than a steadfast, trustworthy person. I regret not getting the message sooner. In his book *The Triumph of Politics,* Stockman needled me about my ignorance on the acid-rain issue— granted, I didn't know acid rain from bee pollen. Later, he accused me of using my influence with Reagan to win a concession for the Canadian government, one of my clients after I left the White House.

GEORGE SHULTZ—In one of those quirks of politics, I remember sitting with Reagan at Pacific Palisades and mentioning Shultz as a prospective secretary of state. Reagan went to the phone, called him, and said he would like to visit with him about coming back to Washington, as a member of the Cabinet. He never mentioned the title, and Shultz assumed he had Treasury in mind. When Reagan hung up the phone, he said to me, puzzled, that Shultz had "no interest" in returning to Washington. It was a misunderstanding, but before it ever got straightened out the job went to Al Haig.

DON REGAN—During a time when I was ill, recovering at home from a kidney failure, Regan came out to the house for what I took to be a courtesy call. He said he had been discussing with Jim Baker a proposal that they switch positions. He had told Baker, he said, that while he wanted to be chief of staff, he would not consider it if Deaver had his sights on the job. I assured him I did not and offered to submit the plan to the president. It was never clear to me, however, why Regan wanted to give up the position he had, with his years of background on Wall Street. Aside from the position of secretary of state or attorney general, the Treasury job entails more enforcement power than any other office in government. It offers more impact on foreign policy, as well as domestic policy, than any title outside of State. In the pecking order, the secretary of state sits on the president's right, the treasury secretary on his left.

"At dinner parties," Regan said, after the move was made, "I sit below the salt now. There are a lot of interesting people there." If I read Regan correctly, which was not always an easy task, he meant he had given up some status, but had pulled his chair up close to the action.

GEORGE BUSH—I admired Bush as a public servant and developed a fondness for him as a strong and caring person who has done a difficult job superbly. We used to get together every morning before our nine o'clock meeting with the president and try to think of a fresh joke or anecdote to tell him. Reagan loves a good story. Bush would call his contacts all over the United States trying to come up with new ones. He gives you his best effort, whatever the task.

I still recall the breakfast the morning the Reagans met the Bushes as the 1976 Republican standard-bearers. Barbara Bush cemented the relationship that morning. As they paused at the door, on the way out, Barbara looked Ronald Reagan in the eye and said, "Governor, let me promise you one thing. We're going to work our tails off for you." There was nothing she could have said, at that moment, that the Reagans would have responded to more.

Before his "hands-off" style was called into public question, the most common analogy pictured Reagan as the chairman of the board. "He's a big-picture man," Meese preferred to say. "He doesn't have to paint that every day. He painted it a long time ago. The fact that someone has reorganized the department of widgets doesn't interest him."

Those words may sound now as if we were making excuses for him. We never saw it that way. Within the staff, the infighting was periodic, but the routine moved smoothly. An average day might go along these lines:

We would arrive at the basement entrance to the West Wing, in separate cars, for a 7:30 A.M. meeting, a working breakfast at Jim Baker's conference table. Filipino stewards from the White House mess quietly served us. Each of us had notes scribbled on scrap paper, but the momentum was Baker's. He always had the longer checklist.

Point by point, we reviewed any overnight foreign developments, pending appointments, the day's legislative agenda, and the current media coverage. By then two lists had been formed: one to be discussed at 8:00 A.M. with the senior staff in the Roosevelt Room, and the other at 8:45 with the president himself in the Oval Office.

Reagan liked a fast track. As soon as one topic had been disposed of, he would say, "Good. What's next?" If he began to tell stories, or his eyes wandered, I would give a discreet signal—a nod, a quick propeller motion with my hand—to cut it off or move on.

My title, as deputy chief of staff, meant little in the context of my obligation to Ronald Reagan. In making decisions, I was able to rely on my sense of his strengths and needs, and of how to budget his exposure to the media. I would not deny that at times I programmed him too much. It is in Reagan's nature and his preference to answer questions. But not all questions are meant to be answered, not if you want to focus a network's attention on a certain event or issue rather than a casual remark dropped by the president as he crosses the White House lawn.

When he broke my no-questions rule, and at times when he did not, the results were unpredictable. Once, he said to the reporters, "I don't take questions at news conferences."

When you get down to it, it is people that make a presidency work, not images. But images help. The trip to the Demilitarized Zone on the border between North and South Korea was a symbolic high point of the Reagan years. Standing there, staring across that buffer zone, drawing the contrast between freedom and oppression, this was what Ronald Reagan did best.

In Normandy, I had a very strong sense that we had put some of the past behind us. I had received a copy of a letter a woman had written to the president before the trip, explaining that her father had always intended to return to Normandy, where he had fought with the 37th Engineer Combat Battalion. But he had died of cancer, and she had vowed to make the pilgrimage for him.

Her name is Lisa Zanatta Henn, twenty-eight, of Millbrae, California. Her father was Peter Robert Zanatta.

I called the letter to the president's attention, and he took it with him to Normandy and then read it to two thousand visitors at the Omaha Beach Memorial, while Lisa Zanatta Henn stood near him:

"I'm going there, Dad," she had written, "and I'll see the beaches and the barricades and the monuments." As he read, the president's voice began to crack. "I'll see the graves and I'll put flowers there just like you wanted to do. I'll never forget what you went through, Dad, nor will I let anyone else forget. And, Dad, I'll always be proud."

The president's eyes brimmed and he had to choke out the final words. Lisa Henn wept openly. The president, incidentally, personally paid her way to Normandy.

Months later, I heard from Kay Graham that she had watched a film of the trip, and she cried at the moment when Reagan and the young woman made eye contact during the reading of the letter. Then, when Reagan finished, the camera pulled back to a couple of veterans, seventy-five-year old guys in their Amvet hats.

I really don't think his reaction has a thing in the world to do with having been an actor. But such moments did bring out the best in Ronald Reagan. At such moments, the world really was his stage.

War Movies

Ronald Reagan never left the American shores during World War II. He never really left Hollywood, where he served as a captain in what was then known as the Army Air Corps.

He was assigned to a squadron that made training films in Culver City, not far from the MGM studios. Dore Schary, the director, commanded the unit, whose ranks included another star, Alan Ladd.

They were known, even to each other, as the "Culver City Commandos."

About his acting, and his military service, Reagan has taken a teasing that ranges from friendly to not quite ferocious. His patriotism, his fondness for war stories, his admiration for those who have worn our country's uniforms are well documented.

In the mid-1980s, a growing number of people seemed willing to believe that for Reagan reality and myth often blur. It has been suggested that he would borrow from his movie roles to give texture to his wartime duties. He was, and is, fond of telling stories about heroic pilots, or POWs who staged daring escapes.

Reagan may have heard the stories firsthand, from the veterans who brought them back. He may have had burned into his mind a scene from the combat footage his unit would sometimes edit. Or, yes, the real acts of courage or horror may have blended with moments from his old films.

Another issue seemed to bother some of his critics: that Reagan wanted people to believe he had seen these deeds, or had somehow brushed the actual events. That suggestion surfaced anew while the president pondered his trip to Bitburg, West Germany, amid an international furor.

But Reagan is a romantic, not an imposter. When he talked about seeing the bodies of Holocaust victims piled like firewood, he may or may not have explained he had been viewing the footage shipped home by the Signal Corps. (He saw this nightmare on film, not in person. That did not mean he saw it less.)

And as he steeled himself to go to Bitburg and face the anger and anguish of the survivors of Nazi barbarity, and of those who fought against it, he remembered watching the unedited black-and-white pictures:

"I remember one shot—I can never forget. There was a building that looked like a warehouse. The floor was entirely carpeted with bodies. And in that film, while we were looking at that, out in the middle of all those bodies, suddenly, slowly one body moved and raised up, a man on his elbow, and tried with his other hand to gesture. He was alone, alive with the dead."

It is a terrible thing to have people accuse you of toying with tragedy. The president tried to deflect the most painful of the criticism by changing the emphasis of the trip; away from the anniversary of the war's end, to a celebration of forty years of peace and alliance.

And so he went.

9
Return
to
Bitburg

I remember a rather barbed tribute to a fellow departing a job under fire, paraphrasing Shakespeare: "Nothing he did in his position became him quite so well as his leaving it."

Well, we would all prefer a big finish, a graceful exit, a happy ending. But it seems safe to say that there were few generous commentaries on my final official service to the presidency of Ronald Reagan.

The trip to Bitburg started out as an afterthought, a minor footnote to the economic summit scheduled in May 1985 among the Western allies. We would be walking through a cemetery, not a minefield. The visit coincided with the fortieth anniversary of the end of the Second World War.

I was going out on a high note. Reagan was near his peak of popularity in the polls. His reelection had resulted in a virtual shutout over Mondale, one of the two biggest landslides in history. The daily press and the weekly news magazines had hailed me as "Magic Mike," and "The Vicar of Visuals."

If I qualified as an expert on anything, it was said to be the staging of a media event; blending the gifts of Ronald Reagan with the proper pageantry. Not everyone looked on this capacity with respect. Chefs who barbecue cows for a living call it selling the sizzle.

But it was part of my job, the part I often enjoyed most. And so my final act was to help arrange the agenda and the coverage of the president's trip to Europe. The furor that came later, some suggested, was the result of my attention being divided, meaning that my mind was already at least partly on the new public-relations firm I would launch as soon as my White House resignation took effect.

Whatever mistakes were made at Bitburg were mine. Let me leave no doubt on that point and move on. But it was not the result of insensitivity, or inattention, or carelessness.

Hindsight is a wonderful tool. I know what went wrong and how the controversy could have been avoided. But when the plans were first laid, no one saw the pitfalls; or, if anyone did, they neglected to point them out.

In February 1985, having convinced the president that the time had come for me to move on, I flew to Europe to work out the details of his European trip, the highlight of which was to be the economic summit in Bonn, West Germany.

A few months earlier, in November, the president had agreed to a vague request by Helmut Kohl, the West German chancellor, to take part in a ceremony marking the friendship, the reconciliation, between our two countries. The obvious and traditional idea, the symbolic visit to a concentration camp, appealed to neither side and was quietly dropped.

There was a sense of projecting an era of hope and a closing of the book on the past. This the camps could not do; they existed as a remembrance of the ghastly deeds that occurred there. No one could or should forget them.

I had the additional factor of Ronald Reagan's nature. He was not at ease with, nor eager to confront, scenes of unrelenting depression. He was at his best when he could touch the nostalgia, the longing in each of us for a more romantic time. You put him near a flag, around uniforms, or in sight of a parade, and he could lift anyone's spirit.

Helmut Kohl suggested a joint visit to the military cemetery at Bitburg, the laying of a wreath to honor the dead of all our armies. We asked the question we always asked on such trips: Was there anything there that might embarrass our president, our country? The answer was no.

We literally could not see the pitfalls. It was February. The graves, most of the markers, were covered by blankets of snow. I added this visit to the itinerary and the wheels were put in motion.

I flew back to Washington with Bitburg fairly well down on my list of concerns. My attention was more tightly focused on assuring that Reagan would not be overscheduled and over-drawn during his weeks abroad, that he was rested and prepared for the economic policy talks. I had not forgotten—Nancy never let me forget—that I had failed to build in enough rest periods on an earlier journey, and Reagan had nodded off while talking to the pope.

The summit was planned for the second week in May. In mid-April, German newspapers carried the story that the cemetery we had selected included the graves not only of ordinary soldiers but also of forty-nine members of the Waffen SS, a branch of the dreaded Nazi guard that ran the death camps.

In Europe, the United States, and the Soviet Union, the out-cry was immediate and bitter. Wounds long unhealed but ig-nored surfaced again. Veterans marched and mailed back their medals. Jewish groups demonstrated and begged the president to back off. No newscast, no edition of any newspaper, was complete without an interview with a person who had lost some-one, or everyone, in the Holocaust.

Those reactions, those emotions, were genuine and for the most part spontaneous. The anguish we saw and heard was pain-ful then, and I do not take it lightly now. But the judgment had been made. The only question was, at what cost would we undo it, or did we take the heat and move ahead?

It is difficult, but not impossible, to defend the trip to the tiny cemetery in the middle of Bitburg. Our intentions were valid, and President Reagan restated them in an interview with Hugh Sidey of *Time* magazine:

"We're not going there in the sense of forgive and forget. What I believe is needed is a recognition of what has been ac-complished in the new Germany, that here is a Germany that is certainly the most democratic regime the German people have ever known. You know, you could see where a country that had done what [the Nazis] did might have bulldozed out of existence

those camps and said, 'Let's pretend it never happened, and
let's never mention it again.'

". . . And now, today, you have a German people who are
our staunchest allies and friends, for 30 years an ally in NATO,
40 years of peace."

This was to have been the theme of the journey, not just the
observance of an anniversary, but the settling of certain debts,
the recognition that the torch had been passed.

But even as the firestorm of controversy engulfed the country,
there were deep divisions on the president's staff. Everyone had
an opinion. But, basically, I felt it was my mess and I had to
clean it up.

One of my first tasks was to keep Pat Buchanan the hell out of it.
He is a tough, talented, outspoken wordsmith, a purist when it
comes to the conservative faith, far enough to the right that he
considers school lunches a subversive plot. Now, as the new communications director in the White House, he would be one of the
people most often whispering in Ronald Reagan's ear. I will say it
again: Reagan does not need anyone to the right of him.

Buchanan argued for a harder line, a bigger gesture, a clearer
defense of the new Germany and virtually an amnesty for the Third
Reich; whatever it took to avoid the appearance that the president
was bending under pressure from Jewish or any other groups.

Once it became clear that the president was not open to suggestions that he cancel or cut back the trip, I knew that what he
said there would in large measure determine how the passage to
Bitburg would be judged. Ken Khachigian, a former Reagan
speechwriter, was brought back to work with Josh Gilder in
crafting the text of what the president would say. The theme was
his own. He wanted to meet the issue squarely. He wanted to
put it in the context of where we had come in forty years.

The country was still in an uproar. The memories of the Nazi
atrocities, the hardships and sacrifices of the war, revived an anger that swept across the generation gap. The issue had esca-
lated into the worst crisis of the Reagan presidency. How could
anyone support us, or understand what we had meant to do?
The trip to Bitburg seemed stupid, or worse, even to those who
had not been born when the SS was doing its obscene work.

On April 19, Helmut Kohl called and personally asked Ronald Reagan not to give in to the critics, not to break the promise Kohl felt had been made to him. We now believed that our relationship with West Germany, and the stability of the Kohl government, depended on our ability to *not* make the situation worse.

Kohl feared we would make last-minute changes that might be taken as an insult to the West German people, and weaken his leadership. He was, after all, the first chancellor of the republic who had grown to manhood in the postwar era.

We inched our way toward a more favorable plan. Advice kept pouring in: Richard Nixon warned Reagan not to retreat. Henry Kissinger called, adding that if we canceled Bitburg enormous damage would be done to America's foreign policy.

The options did not seem very attractive. We could cut our losses, and quiet the uproar, but risk the credibility of Ronald Reagan and his administration. Or we could ride it out, and hope that by remaining consistent, by once again promoting Reagan as a man of conviction, right or wrong, we would at least gain a standoff.

This was one of those periods when no one seemed to be talking about anything else. The economy, Nicaragua, everything else had been moved to the back burner. The president was hurting. I felt like falling on my sword. And the disposition of neither of us was helped by the fact that the criticism had led to my first serious conflict with Nancy Reagan.

I could not recall our ever before having been on opposite sides of an issue. But now she was convinced that I had ruined her husband's presidency, and perhaps the rest of his life. We had a very painful, emotional confrontation. I let her finish and said, "Nancy, it's done. If going into a panic would help, I'd panic. But I'm trying to do my damnedest to make the best of a very difficult situation. Let me get on with it, please."

If I had injured the president, she knew I had not done so out of indifference, or any ambition of my own. I had to cut off the conversation, knowing that outside my office were five or six people waiting to help me put the pieces back together. So for me the best course was the one I had always tried to take with her: to be direct and truthful. *I made a mistake. Now I was trying to fix it.* Nancy nodded her head and, without a word, walked out.

Her attitude was that the damage had been done. Almost to the last minute, she insisted the trip should be canceled. She said so to me. She said so to her husband. I have never, not in the years I have known them, seen the Reagans engage in a no-holds-barred argument. She may push to a point where he slams a table with his hand, or throws down a fountain pen, but I doubt that they have ever exchanged the really ugly words not uncommon to most marriages. This could reflect what a very private couple they are, or it could mean that they belong in the *Guinness Book of World Records* or the Smithsonian.

In this case, it ended when the president said: "Nancy, I simply don't believe you're right and I'm not going to change my mind." She pressed him no further.

On the early part of the trip, she was almost physically ill. I felt for her deeply.

I had decided to add a side trip to a concentration camp after all, the one at Bergen-Belsen. The move exposed us to charges of flip-flopping, and reeked of politics, but our objective now was to balance Bitburg, not reject it.

The ceremony would be brief, and clean, almost sterile, and there would be no speeches. But canceling the trip never had been a serious option in the mind of Ronald Reagan (nor in mine). He was not going to abandon Helmut Kohl or embarrass the West German nation. While far from immune to public sentiment, Reagan is one of those stubborn individuals who hardens when he feels pressured.

I was to fly back to Germany twenty-four hours before the Reagans made their departure. An hour before my flight was to leave from Andrews Air Force Base, at six o'clock, the president called me into the Oval Office. He said, "I know you and Nancy have been talking. But I don't want to change these plans one bit. What we are doing is right and will go down in the history books as right."

One reason he felt that way was an unexpected turn of fortune that had occurred earlier in the day, had just fallen into my lap. I was sitting at my desk, still flogging myself, trying to think if there was anything else we could do. My secretary buzzed me and said that there was a Matt Ridgway on the phone. I said I didn't know any Matt Ridgway.

There was a pause and she came back on the line: "He says he is *General* Matthew Ridgway."

I said, "My God, I didn't know he was still alive."

I grabbed the phone and heard him say, "Mr. Deaver, this is Matt Ridgway."

I said, "Yes, sir."

He said, "I am a soldier and I have never done anything political in my life. But it appears to me that my commander in chief is in trouble and I would like to help. I would like to lay that wreath in Bitburg for him. I am the last living four-star general who was involved in the European theater."

I asked if I could put him on hold for a moment and I walked next door, into the Oval Office, and said, "Mr. President, you are not going to believe this. But Matthew Ridgway is on the phone and he has offered to lay the wreath at Bitburg for you so you won't have to do it."

Of course, one of the lingering and most bitter complaints had been directed at the prospect of the president of the United States appearing to honor the soil that contained the remains of the Nazi SS. Ridgway, now ninety, had led the U.S. 82nd Airborne Division in action against the enemy.

The president punched the lighted button on his phone and said, "General, this is Ron Reagan. Mike Deaver just told me what you want to do and I won't let you. But I will agree to our laying that wreath together."

So the cast was expanded. I flew over to Bonn and met with Helmut Kohl. At the end of our conversation, I advised him that the president was bringing Matthew Ridgway with him and would like the chancellor to bring one of his generals in the same spirit. Kohl and his aides began to chatter in German, and he looked at me and said, "Yes, we have someone."

He gave me the name: General Johannes Steinhoff. I said, "Sir, with all due respect, you better snake-check that son of a bitch for everything he's worth."

Steinhoff, then seventy-one, turned out to be a Luftwaffe ace, who had been assigned to Ridgway's NATO staff after the war.

The day dawned damp and gray and the pilgrimage began at Bergen-Belsen. The president, hand in hand with Nancy, walked through the museum with row after row of horrifying photographs of pits filled with bones and piles of naked corpses and those barely living, hollow-eyed and skeletal, liberated by American troops in the spring of 1945. The dead of Bergen-Belsen included a Dutch schoolgirl named Anne Frank.

Here Reagan spoke:

"Here lie people—Jews—whose death was inflicted for no reason other than their very existence. Their pain was borne only because of who they were and because of the God in their prayers. . . .

"For year after year, until Hitler and his evil were destroyed, hell yawned forth its awful contents. People were brought here for no other purpose but to suffer and die. To go unfed when hungry, uncared for when sick, tortured when the whim struck—and left to have misery consume them when all there was around them was misery. . . .

"Here, death ruled. But we have learned something as well. Because of what happened, we found that death cannot rule forever. . . . We are here because humanity refuses to accept that freedom, or the spirit of man, can ever be extinguished. We are here to commemorate that life triumphed over the tragedy and the death of the Holocaust—overcame the suffering, the sickness, the testing and, yes, the gassings. We're here today to confirm that the horror cannot outlast hope. . . .

"Out of the ashes—hope, and from all the pain, promise. So much of this is symbolized today by the fact that most of the leadership of free Germany is represented here today. Chancellor Kohl, you and your countrymen have made real the renewal that had to happen. Your nation and the German people have been strong and resolute in your willingness to confront and condemn the acts of a hated regime of the past. This reflects the courage of your people and their devotion to freedom and justice since the war.

"Think how far we have come from that time when despair

made these tragic victims wonder if anything could survive. . . . We can understand that, when we see what is around us—all these children of God, under bleak and lifeless mounds, the plainness of which does not even hint at the unspeakable acts that created them. Here they lie. Never to hope. Never to pray. Never to love. Never to heal. Never to laugh. Never to cry . . .

"We are all witnesses. We share the glistening hope that rests in every human soul. Hope leads us—if we are prepared to trust it—toward what our President Lincoln called "the better angels of our nature." And, then, rising above all this cruelty—out of this tragic and nightmarish time—beyond the anguish, the pain and the suffering for all time, we can and must pledge:

"Never again."

We flew to Bitburg, and from the airport a motorcade carried us through the open countryside, past the demonstrators and into the cemetery. The graves, with flat markers, were arranged in thirty-two rows, with flowers placed at each stone.

The official party followed a brick walkway, taking care to avoid the area where the Waffen SS men were buried. Reagan and Kohl stopped at the main memorial, where two tall wreaths had been placed against a gray wall. With the generals standing at attention behind them, each touched a wreath and stepped back.

A lone German army bugler played an ode to lost soldiers, "Ich Hatt' Einen Kameraden" ("I Had a Comrade"). Reagan and Kohl shook hands with the honor guard, and the mayor of Bitburg, and the surviving relatives of German soldiers who had taken part in the plot to kill Hitler.

Eight minutes after it had entered the cemetery, the motorcade was on its way to the airport. And then the president spoke again, of his feelings about both the camp at Bergen-Belsen and the cemetery at Bitburg:

"No one could visit there without deep and conflicting emotions. I felt great sadness that history could be filled with such waste, destruction, and evil. But my heart was also lifted by the knowledge that from the ashes has come hope and from the terrors of the past we have built forty years of peace, freedom, and reconciliation among our nations.

"We cannot undo the crimes and wars of yesterday, nor call

the millions back to life. But we can give meaning to the past by learning its lessons and making a better future. We can let our pain drive us to greater efforts to heal humanity's suffering.''

A German military band played "The Star-Spangled Banner," and our U.S. Air Force musicians followed with the West German anthem. Kohl thanked Reagan "as a friend, for taking this step, for having made that march together with me."

The historians will tell us whether the president changed any minds or hearts, or whether the visit to Bitburg damaged his reputation and dishonored the memory of those who fought and died forty years earlier. My instinct tells me that Bitburg will be remembered for a gesture well meant and, against deep-rooted resistance, well timed.

"This visit has stirred many emotions in the American and German people, too," he acknowledged. "Some old wounds have been reopened and this I regret very much, because this should be a time of healing.

"To the veterans and families of American servicemen who still carry the scars and feel the painful losses of that war . . . and to those who survived the Holocaust . . . [who] are worried that reconciliation means forgetting. I promise you, we will never forget."

For all of the grim images and the raw, sobering, emotional scars, most of us left Germany lighter in mood than when we came. The president had endured, had in my mind *overcome* barriers that some feared, or hoped, would endanger his authority.

I can't say for certain, not yet, that we turned a bad situation into one with potential. But that was, and is, my hope.

He made connections that he felt driven to make. In his speech at the airport, he echoed the mood of John F. Kennedy's ringing words, in 1963: *"Ich bin ein Berliner."* He said to the hundred or so on the tarmac, and to the millions who might yet hear around the globe:

"Today freedom-loving people . . . must say, 'I am a Jew in a world still threatened by antisemitism. I am an Afghan and I am a prisoner of the gulag. I am a refugee in a crowded boat foundering off the coast of Vietnam. I am a Laotian, a Cambodian, a Cuban, and a Miskito Indian in Nicaragua. I, too, am a . . . victim of totalitarianism."

It had been hard, mean sledding. There is no dignified way to debate those who have been through the fire, such as Elie Wiesel, the writer and scholar who was a child in the camps and lost his family there, who received a Presidential Medal of Freedom and made a deeply moving appeal on national television for Reagan to cancel the ceremony at Bitburg. In the end, one would not try to argue with them.

The protests had grown more shrill when the president had said that the young German soldiers buried there were as much victims of the Nazi ideology as the victims of the Holocaust. They were troubling words and poorly expressed. He meant only to make the point that not every German was a Nazi, not every reluctant young soldier a war criminal. Some of them died in a cause they did not support or understand.

And now it was a time to cleanse the old wounds, the old hatreds. That may have been too idealistic a goal. But that was Reagan. And he pulled us out of a ditch to nearly bring it off. We may still find that he did. At the least, he had taken an explosive and emotional situation and met it with skill and honesty.

One thing I have learned and relearned about Ronald Reagan: When he believes he is morally right on a stand, there is hell getting him off it. Bitburg may or may not have been the right location for the symbolism we had in mind. But the trip was about reconciliation and an alliance for the future, and it was crucial that those goals not be lost in the clamor.

I want to be careful not to reduce the Bitburg episode to an exercise in public relations. But the gestures we made there did not warrant what I regarded as the overreaction of international opinion. No one in his right mind would try to play down the feelings of horror that are a legacy of World War II. There is no pairing of words any bigger or more tragic. There is no humor here, no lightness. But if we fail to seek out the hope, we are left only with the inhumanity.

I felt relief and even a touch of satisfaction as I cleaned out my desk at the White House some weeks later. My send-off to the private sector had turned out to be a a stormy one—although I had no reason to suspect I would soon encounter a storm of my own. But after the anguish of Bitburg had passed, and the media had moved on to other worries and distractions, I was left with a lingering memory.

Our motorcade had left Bergen-Belsen, where ten thousand bodies had been buried in eleven common graves, under mounds of earth planted with heather. We had ended the ceremonies at Bitburg, where German and American troops exchanged the colors.

I was already in my seat on Air Force One, which was parked on a ramp overlooking the cemetery. And as the chancellor spoke, and the president spoke, I looked out my window and could not contain a smile at what I saw there,

There were General Matthew Ridgway, ninety, and General Johannes Steinhoff, seventy-one, standing side by side, their hands lightly touching at the fingertips.

The Pilgrimage

The president loves a shaggy-dog story. So I provided him with one.

I had just returned from Portugal in the autumn of 1984, having stopped there after visits to Spain and Germany. It was on this same swing that the initial planning for the trip to Bitburg had begun. The times were serious and the approach was businesslike, but no crisis had yet appeared on the horizon.

On my return to Washington, I made my report to a meeting attended by the president, George Bush, George Shultz, and Bud McFarlane, then the national security adviser.

The heavyweights were out because of a controversy that had developed in Spain. One of our CIA agents had been caught taking pictures outside the Spanish prime minister's home, and he had been expelled from the country. There was then talk of the president's visit being canceled.

"They know you're his friend and personal representative," our ambassador said, after briefing me. "You may be the only one who can save the visit."

A meeting was hastily arranged with the foreign minister, but my apologies seemed to bounce off him until I blurted out, entirely ad lib, "These CIA people are assholes to have done such a thing."

There were several hasty exchanges in Spanish with the minister's aides, and smiles around the room. Then the ambassador and I were excused. Two hours later, word arrived that the trip was back on. It was then that the ambassador confided that in certain Latin circles, profanity was held in high regard as evidence of sincerity.

I had scored a diplomatic success of sorts, and the mood of the White House meeting instantly became lighter. Someone asked about my trip to Portugal. I had traveled to all the locations where the official meetings would be held, frankly searching for a spot that would offer a strong background for pictures of the president. One of my hosts suggested the Shrine of Fatima. We checked out a helicopter, flew down to the village, and scouted the area.

At the risk of sounding disrespectful, I must say the area was bleak and barren and it became clear that the shrine would not work as a photo site. Of course, I hasten to concede that this was never a part of its original design.

But as I began to describe the scene, for reasons I cannot at all explain, I found myself warming to the story. I reminded them—the president and vice-president of the United States, the secretary of state and the national security adviser—that the shrine was where, in the 1920s, a vision of the Virgin Mary had supposedly appeared to three young shepherd girls and given them a message to deliver to whoever was the pope in the year 1960.

Indeed, the message had been delivered and was said to be so powerful, so filled with portent, it has never been revealed.

I must pause to explain that Ronald Reagan is nuts for religious phenomena. He reads whatever he gets his hands on, watches any movie or television show that deals with the subject.

He kept leaning farther across his desk as I went on:

"One of the shepherdesses is still alive, in her nineties, in a hospital in Fatima. I received word that she had heard that a representative of the American government was there, and she had asked to see me."

Now I had the total attention of everyone in the room. No one else spoke. The business of running the country could wait. "I was ushered into her room," I told them, "and there was this frail, shrunken little woman, her dark eyes holding me. In a faint voice, in English, she motioned me to her side and asked me to bend over her, and she would tell me the message.

"I stood there and wondered to myself, why me? Of all people, why me?"

Now Reagan was on the edge of his seat and he broke in, impatiently. "Well, what was the message?"

I said, "She told me that the Virgin had said to her, 'In 1960, tell the pope that someday . . . a young actor named Ronald Reagan will visit this site.'"

I received the unanimous groan I undoubtedly deserved. But they all bit, all fell for it. There really is no moral to the story, except that even within the walls of great power, you can't always take yourselves seriously.

And, in the end, Ronald Reagan did not visit the site.

10
Over
the
Wall

Sooner or later, anyone who considers working for the federal government must ask these two questions: 1) How can I leave all the fine and familiar things at home to live in Washington, and 2) having gone, and had my brush with the people who hold the power, how can I give it up?

This assumes, of course, that the second choice is your own.

This is the one overriding reality of life in the White House. From the first day you step inside to begin the job, you are in the process of leaving it. The only question is how.

I do not intend to go on and on about the headaches and anguish of a career I loved. But the simple truth is, I never really worked for anyone except Ronald Reagan, after my one year as a sales trainee for IBM. I wince, as others must, when I read of someone bailing out of a job for one that pays two or three times as much and saying nobly, "I did it all for the family."

And yet, in my mind, there is no question that my family felt they rated somewhere behind the Reagans in the long and sometimes bumpy ride from Sacramento to Washington. Those were years of putting things off, of never quite being able to afford the things we wanted.

It grew harder each year to break away from the kind of bond I believe we had forged. After a while, I no longer wanted to break away.

I came very close to doing so after the 1980 election. I wrestled with the question of going to Washington or returning to my public-relations firm in Los Angeles. Carolyn came down hard on the side of staying in California. She definitely did not have Potomac fever.

After days of debating with myself, of doing a mental hat dance, I walked into the governor's office, thanked him for everything, and said I would not be making the move with the rest of the team. He seemed to accept it. I called Carolyn and said, "I'm coming home . . . to stay."

When she was sure I meant it, she decided to break out a bottle of 1968 Heitz Chardonnay we had been saving, the finest white wine made in America. We had just settled ourselves on the patio when the phone rang.

I went into the house to answer it. Ronald Reagan was on the other end. "I know how you feel," he said. "But I need you. Come on back with me for one year. Give it that much at least, and see how it goes."

He had said the magic words. I could not resist—can anyone?—a freshly elected president saying, "I need you." When I walked back out to the yard, I didn't have to say a thing. Carolyn had tears streaking her cheeks. She knew what the call was about and what the answer would be. It confirmed a story she had already read in the paper. Until that moment, I thought the story was wrong.

We put away the wine. I never imagined then what a hard adjustment the move would be for her. Two months after we arrived in Washington, her father died. She did not shake off the shock easily, and still had to cope with the excessive Washington social demands and a degree of attention neither of us had known. The first year or two, we received some fifty invitations a week. I used to joke that we wore formal clothes so often that my son, Blair, thought "black tie" was the name of a restaurant.

Still, a transformation took place. About the time I knew I had to get out on my own, we both realized we had planted roots in Washington. It had become our home. Whatever I did, whenever I did it, we were not going to move back to the West Coast, not in the near future.

There is just no town on earth quite like Washington. Where else can you hear "The Star-Spangled Banner" four times a day? When you work at the White House, in time you take for granted the protocol and the social whirl. But I never drove through the White House gates in the morning without getting a little chill. Nor could I resist the chance to pause, and reflect, at the Tomb of the Unknown Soldier or the Washington Monument.

I hear people brag about living in the city all their lives and never visiting those shrines unless they have a guest to show around. How sad. They are missing out on the best gift this country has to offer—heritage.

I look back on the five years I spent in the White House as just one long adrenaline rush. I experienced more emotional highs and lows in one day than most people do in a lifetime.

But by January 1985, with the reelection behind us, I knew I had to get out. I had landed in the hospital with a kidney failure, complicated by high blood pressure, and I knew I could not physically endure four more years.

My own experience makes me appreciate even more that Ronald Reagan has taken so much in stride. I don't mean this in a boastful way, but I was able to relieve him of certain stresses, and there was no one else to take a hand-off from me. Whenever Carolyn got upset with me, feeling that I was making the dependence greater than it needed to be, I would tell her: "But you don't understand. I'm the only guy who can help this man in this way." And so I truly believed. He could leave a problem or a confidence with me, even a personal one, and go merrily on to other matters. And I was left with this pressure—not to let him down, not to embarrass him, not to reveal unintentionally what was said in a private and trusting moment.

At such times, I felt as if I had swallowed an anchor. With his upbeat and placid nature, Reagan did not get ulcers. But he was a carrier.

I was fortunate to the degree that I have been most of my life

a disciplined person. I don't see how the disorganized can survive in high government positions, with all the scheduling, the
endless need to concentrate.

I don't know how Ed Meese manages, but he does, and Ed is
famous for his clutter. There are always so many documents and
letters on his desk, roaches could be having orgies in there and
no one would know it.

There was no special reason, nothing dramatic, that led me to
enter the president's office on the day I did, and give him my
notice. After all, I had been talking about it for five years.
There had been newspaper articles speculating that I would
leave. But I knew Carolyn would not believe it until the day
the limo stopped coming to deliver me to 1600 Pennsylvania
Avenue.

When I was certain I would not change my mind, the first
thing I did was call Nancy Reagan. She was in the truest sense of
the phrase my best friend. There was nothing I could not talk to
her about, nothing I did not talk to her about. I asked if I could
stop by the residence and see her. When I said I felt it was my
time to leave, she asked me to stay just one more year.

I would have laughed if I could have gotten my mouth to
work. I said, "Nancy, that's what I always say to the people who
have come to me in the past. I can't. I have to leave." We probably talked for an hour, and then I went to the Oval Office to
tell the president.

In everyone's life there is a time to close the books on whatever has been your special cause or special friendship. And no
matter how often you hear or read about it, or go through it
yourself, it never gets easier.

I had watched people go into his office year after year and say
their good-byes. I thought he was always wonderful about it,
very understanding and unselfish. Now it was my turn. We got
through the preliminaries and he said, "You know, Mike, I like
to think I'm the only indispensable person around here, but the
truth is . . ."

I put up my hand, like a stop sign, and broke in: "Please,
Ron," and I think it was the only time in my life I had called
him Ron, "don't say whatever you were going to say. Don't do

that to me." I might have used the more familiar term when I referred to him at home or among friends, but never to his face. From the first day I had worked for him, until that moment, it had been "Governor" or "Mr. President." Only then, in the first stage of my leave-taking, did I allow myself the license of alluding to the personal bond that was there.

We both knew I would be around another few months. There was still the Bitburg trip to plan, of course. I eased out of there, and my next stop was Jim Baker's office. Then I called Larry Speakes and said I wanted my resignation announced at one o'clock. The quicker the word got out, the less likely that my mind could be changed. I called Carolyn before I left the White House. While I was en route, she heard it on TV. And *that* made it official.

When I walked into the house, she and the kids were waiting for me. Amanda chirped, "Mom, we won, we won."

Blair said, "I guess this means we won't be invited back to the White House."

Mine was not a decision made in anger or frustration or on impulse. It just seemed the right time. I was sure of it when, three weeks later, I found out how shaky my health was.

I can't honestly say how much of the problem was due to poor habits, and how much to the pressures of the job, of being the mediator, the man in the middle so often. I had traveled constantly—three times to Asia, twice to Europe. A fairly madcap schedule for a guy with a history of hypertension. The doctors kept adjusting my medication to get my blood pressure down to a reasonable level.

From boyhood on, I was cursed with a system that was allergic to just about everything, including prosperity, it often seemed. I had a wide array of sinus allergies and was allergic to penicillin. The week before the second Reagan inauguration, I caught what I thought was the flu, and I went to bed in one of those moods where you think that you might get better, but you will never get well.

I was still taking my blood-pressure medication.

From this point, most of what I will describe I learned from other people. Much of it is gone from my memory. But sometime Saturday, the day before the private swearing-in ceremony, I called my driver and said, "Les, where are you?

He said, "What do you mean?"

I said, "I have to be in the parade. You ought to be here right now."

He said, "The parade isn't until Monday."

I said, "Don't argue with me. Just get over here."

Carolyn was then on the board of a private art museum. He called her office and said he had just had a very odd conversation with me. She dismissed it, thinking it was just a symptom of my feeling poorly.

That night she slept in the guest bedroom on our third floor because of my restlessness. I woke her during the night and said, "You have to go downstairs and ice that angel-food cake."

Her eyes were suddenly owlish. "What angel-food cake?"

"There's an angel-food cake in the refrigerator, and it will dry out if you don't ice it."

Carolyn didn't know what to think. A stroke? Alzheimer's disease? She burst out crying. I responded by saying, "Aw, it's no big deal. I'll ice it myself."

The next morning I insisted on going to the private swearing-in ceremony, the first any president had ever had. Without my knowing, Carolyn had contacted a doctor after my weird episode during the night. But she allowed me to go to the ceremony, bundled up heavily against the cold.

I walked into the East Room of the White House and there was a sudden hush. Jim Baker walked over and said, "My God, Mike, what's wrong? You look awful."

I said it was nothing, just a touch of flu.

But Baker stared at me hard. "You look like my first wife did," he said, "three days before she died." He was really frightened for me.

Then Nancy came over and flat ordered me to "get yourself to a hospital. I mean right now."

Again, I said, "It's okay. I just have the flu."

My driver and Carolyn helped walk me to the car. I turned to Carolyn and said, "Dammit, you make me feel like I'm Averell

Harriman," who was then ninety or so and probably no more feeble than I appeared at that moment.

We drove home, and when I walked in a friend, Tom Magovern, was waiting for me. He took one look and said, "We're going to the hospital."

I said, "Why the hell do people keep wanting to put me in the hospital?"

Tom asked, "Have you looked in the mirror recently?"

As a matter of fact, I had not.

"The whole left side of your face is sagging," he said.

When I checked in a neurologist was waiting to examine me. I started to ask him a question and he said, "Shut up and count backwards from one hundred." I got as far as ninety-six and stopped. My mind had gone blank. I didn't know what was happening, but fear went through me as if I had been poked with an electrical cattle prod.

They took a brain scan and did a spinal tap, thinking I might have a brain tumor. What I did not know then was the effect on your neurological system when you suffer a kidney failure—which I had. It turned out that my body could not tolerate the medication I had been taking.

The tests lasted three or four hours before the doctors could be certain of the diagnosis. They were going to start me on dialysis the next morning. The prospect was that I would be on dialysis the rest of my life.

The next day the doctor contacted my older brother, Bill, about the possibility of his being the donor for a kidney transplant. In judging the ability of the kidneys to function, the doctors measure the capacity from 1 (life-threatening) to 100 (full). Mine was at 11.

They started me on liquids, gallons of liquids, all night long. Body functions do not make for glad reading, but you do think about them when there is a risk of losing them. They tracked my liquid intake against my urine, and in the morning my count had gone up a half point. They decided to wait a day to start the dialysis.

Monday came. I had missed the parade. But my kidney capac-

ity had started to increase; they had overcome the medication to
flush themselves out. The machines would not be needed. Tom
Magovern told me if I had waited another twenty-four hours, I
might have been beyond help.

This experience, as the shooting of the president and the near
death of Jim Brady had done earlier, made me look again at the
priorities of life. This time the brush with mortality had been my
own. If I had harbored even the slightest doubt before, I knew
now I had been right to cut the cord.

It is not an exclusive American trait, but most of us do not
exit well. We see the evidence everywhere, people lingering in
doorways at a party, following a car as it backs out the drive, the
unconscious reenactment of man's inability to say good-bye.

It is harder, I think, on those who have led a public life. You
miss feeling important, getting close to the power, to the center
of the stage. Performers are not alone in wanting to take the
stage with them or see the production shut down.

I knew I would miss the White House, especially the closeness
to Ronald and Nancy Reagan. Giving up that relationship—if
some thought I was a surrogate son, I certainly never objected—
was the hardest thing I have ever done. But I wished my suc-
cessors well. The thought of being eclipsed or forgotten held no
pain against the possibility of other forces preventing the president from carrying out his programs.

You fight it every day in Washington, the battle to remain
normal, to be decent. I can remember Carolyn laughing, telling
a reporter: "These hands that shook the hand of Queen Beatrix
vacuumed the house just an hour ago."

She assured me she picked up the freshest gossip in town at
the Georgetown Safeway store. She even overheard my name
mentioned one day while picking over the produce. "I've never
seen so many people so well turned out at a market," she said.
She promised to take me with her when I was available some
Saturday, if I promised to dress up.

The moments of satisfaction far outweigh any regrets I carried
with me from the White House. But I still have twinges, and
wish I could take back the statement I once made about how
hard it was for our family to live on my salary. It was then
$60,662 a year.

Through a window brightly

Not necessarily the news

Flight plan

Dress for success

They all laughed . . . including Prince Philip.

The gorilla caper

With Ed Meese and Bud McFarlane, welcoming Emperor Hirohito to the White House

My good-bye in the Rose Garden

Dear Mike
Merry Christmas and love
Nancy

We received letters from people offering to send us a case of dog food to live on. And I understand that reaction. My complaint was not one with which the average family could empathize.

It hardly matters that the remark was made in what I thought was a social lunch with two reporters who were friends of mine. The quote made the networks and was widely circulated in print. I don't think I have lived it down to this day. I remember when Nelson Rockefeller was being briefed after his nomination for vice-president. He was told he needed to show some sensitivity to the inflation that was killing the earning power of so many Americans.

Rockefeller said he certainly understood. "I'm feeling the effect of inflation myself," he said, "and if I'm feeling it, just think about that poor stiff out there making fifty thousand dollars a year."

I guess my comment had that kind of ring. And there is no point in trying to defend it now. I can only say that anyone who lives comfortably anywhere else in America, on one salary, will be in debt at the same figure in Washington.

My departure marked a virtual clean sweep of the original Reagan management team. Baker was at Treasury, Meese was soon to be the attorney general. Bill Clark came and went twice, and had returned to the tranquillity of his California ranch. Lyn Nofziger and Richard Allen were back in the private sector.

I have no illusions about being a figure of historical interest. I do not have a fancy epitaph to offer, although I would settle for being thought of as someone who did his best, and gave his all, to help a friend.

On the other hand, you do wonder. Once, Carolyn and I drove home after spending a day on a farm with people who had served in four administrations, both Democratic and Republican. I was fascinated by the stories, the range of experience they represented. I said to Carolyn, "Do you suppose ten years from now people are going to be sitting around talking about what *we* did right and *we* did wrong?"

At such moments, one does tend to feel nostalgic. I was a witness at some of the major world events of my time, and that alone is a fairly impressive statement for a one-time fraternity piano player. In truth, I probably could have been happy working as a musician in clubs and lounges. It is not a bad life, if putting food on the table is not a major consideration.

I can honestly say that I never felt uncomfortable around the wealthy friends of the Reagans, or self-conscious about being the least monied person in the room. I respected the fact that these were people who, for the most part, made their fortunes. They did not inherit them. Nor did I feel any envy. No amount of money could have bought the experiences I had.

My exposure to the Reagans did give me an appreciation for good things, a fine painting, the best piano. One of the great luxuries I allowed myself, after I had launched my own consulting business, was to buy the ultimate in pianos, the Busendorfer, made in Vienna. It was delivered on Christmas Eve of 1985. The cost is not quite twice that of a Steinway.

A few days later, I encountered William F. Buckley, and confided proudly that I had just gotten a Busendorfer. "Ah," he said, in that voice like fur, "how wonderful for you. I have two of them."

I have had people ask me if I am a lawyer, and if I ever had a desire to run for office. The answer in both cases is no. I tell them if I had been a lawyer, by now I would at least have been a superior-court judge.

When I took my first political job in the 1960s, I was no starry-eyed idealist. Nor would I be classified as one when I left Ronald Reagan's White House twenty years later. But I am proud of what we accomplished there, and still moved by some of the moments I carried with me.

How well I got to know Ronald Reagan, what I feel about him, I measure now in a couple of vignettes:

• When I was a second-echelon aide in 1967 to the then governor of California, I helped enlist his support for a wildlife-conservation bill. On the day of the decision, I had a wild-duck lunch catered in Reagan's office.
• The day after the attempt on Reagan's life, acutely aware of the gloom and distress that hung over the White House, I or-

dered every arrangement of dried flowers in the West Wing removed. They had been left over from the Carter administration.
I had them replaced with freshly potted daffodils and tulips. It
may sound insignificant, but instantly spirits seemed to brighten.

In whatever I did, I began with the assurance that it was hard
to make Ronald Reagan look bad. I do not mean to sound
boastful, or petty, if I point out that others, in his second term,
found the task not nearly as hard.

It seems pretentious to say that we made a good team, much
less to try to explain why. We shared some basic, down-home
American values, a love of the outdoors and of singing around a
piano. Out of that camaraderie grew an unusual closeness.

For a fellow who knew his first fame and money as an actor, I
found Reagan to be remarkably free of poses. The ham in him
would surface in a setting made for amateurs. Reagan loves the
big-band sound of the 1950s, but there is hardly any music he
can resist, save the really hard-metal sound.

It is fun to watch him around a piano because he sings all the
words, whether the song is "Shine On, Harvest Moon" or
"Strangers in the Night" or "The Battle Hymn of the Republic."
You listen for the voices, you look around, and Ronald Reagan
is always the one singing his heart out. At a banquet, or a meeting of some civic club, he is the first to grab the sheet music and
try out the words.

One of the photographs I cherish most from these years is one
of me at the piano with the president leaning over the keyboard.
The inscription says: "Dear Mike, One more chorus of 'Spring-
time in the Rockies,' and this time use the black keys, too."

The most reassuring part of Washington life to me was, and
still is, the ability of those with opposing opinions to drop their
armor and see each other as honorable people. It is the one
essential in making certain that our system survives.

Such a moment is still vivid in my mind. The president invited
Tip O'Neill to lunch at the White House to celebrate the birthday of the speaker of the House. There were just the three of us
in the private dining room upstairs.

For about an hour they sat there and swapped Irish folk stories and jokes. Here were two elders from the same background, two of the most powerful men in the world, and I watched them walk out of the dining room arm in arm.

Back in the Oval Office, Reagan ordered champagne, which I had never seen him do after lunch. He raised his glass and proposed a toast:

"Tip, if I had a ticket to heaven and you didn't have one, too, I would give mine away and go to hell with you."

O'Neill, with that classical Irish face and the shock of white hair, lifted his glass: "Old pal, old friend," and they drank one to the other.

And you knew that, ten minutes after the refreshments were finished and the good-byes had been said, they would be at each other's throats all over again.

It is the American way. For all the flash floods and eruptions, I can testify that somehow it works.

The Trouble Shooter

The longer you stay in politics, the greater the risk that you will begin to think you are invincible. The hurdles, the potholes, the traps that snare others can't happen to you.

The truth is, I had seen mighty little corruption during twenty years in public service. I had deflected some situations, and fired a few fellows for "poor judgment." I had fired a few more for appearing to get too close to the cookie jar. But in all those years I had observed no more than four or five cases of actual corruption. I had learned how to recognize the signs when I saw them, and knew, or should have known, how to stay out of harm's way.

Overall, my opinion of the political system was healthier than most people's, dating back to my first job in the governor's office in California. I was a kind of ombudsman, dealing with all the various departments and agencies. Problems, Inc. Part of my job was to screen the people who wanted to see the governor.

One day I received a fellow who was in the trucking business, who said he was having terrible problems with the labor commissioner. According to his story, the commissioner had been forcing him to make payments that he felt were unfair, if not illegal, and he was in danger of being put out of business. In addition, his mother had suffered a heart attack.

I fell for it and, sharing his indignation, picked up the phone in front of him and called my contact in the labor department, Bill Hern. Knowing I was a twenty-nine-year-old rookie, Hern asked, "Mike, is this guy sitting in your office now?"

I said, "Yes."

He said, "Get him out of there. Quick. That guy is connected with the Mafia."

Hanging up the phone, I smiled, asked him to put everything he told me in a letter and assured him we would take care of it. His name had meant nothing to me then. It did later. He was Jimmy Fratianno, known as Jimmy the Weasel, and his name was one of those tossed around when the CIA toyed with a wild scheme to hire a hit man to kill Fidel Castro.

My education had only just begun.

11

The Rise

and

Fall

On a morning in late February 1986, I stopped at a newstand on my way to the office and picked up a copy of *Time* magazine. The face on the cover was my own. The photograph showed me sitting in the back of a chauffeur-driven Lincoln Town Car, talking on a cellular phone.

In large print, the cover line read: WHO'S THIS MAN CALLING? And, in smaller type, came the teaser: "Influence peddling in Washington." In the photo caption, I was identified as "Lobbyist Michael Deaver."

The car was theirs. Mine was in the shop, so the editors at *Time* thoughtfully provided a replacement. No matter. I drove a silver-gray Jaguar at the time, so if the idea was to suggest style or power or a certain ambience, the symbol chosen hardly mattered.

Still, with my first glance at the cover came a thought as subtle as a two-by-four: *"I have been had."* Not by the magazine, nor by enemies unseen, but by my own failure to do for myself what I had always, faithfully, tried to do for my clients: think out every angle and detail, and shelter them as much as possible from criticism or embarrassment.

My reaction was complicated by the fact that for most of the past twenty years I had concentrated on one client, Ronald Wilson Reagan. That cover photo, and the message it conveyed, I knew would not be helpful to either one of us.

Not long after I arrived at my office, Nancy Reagan was on the phone. "Mike," she said, "you made a big mistake. I think you are going to regret posing for that photograph."

She was telling me that I had violated one of the first rules of the Washington game: Try not to have too much success too soon. If you do, then be discreet; otherwise someone will think you are enjoying it.

The article in that issue of *Time,* the parts that applied to me, were not really unflattering or damaging. But the picture, the car, the phone, the caption, well, that was like bleeding in front of a shark.

But I am getting ahead of the story. I am not exactly sure how, or why, but it began with acid rain.

I cannot imagine a less promising chore than to defend yourself in the pages of a book, at least without coming off as self-serving, bitter, or paranoid. What rushes to mind is the famous Abe Lincoln story about the man who was tarred and feathered and run out of town. "If it wasn't for the honor," Lincoln quoted the man, "I'd just as soon walk."

Except for the honor, I would just as soon not have been the first person ever indicted by a special prosecutor, in the six such cases investigated since Watergate. And here is how I got there:

When I established my own company, Michael K. Deaver and Associates, I never thought of or described it as some high-powered lobbying outfit. With a small staff of key people who knew how the federal system worked, we hoped to offer management strategies to clients who needed a Washington presence.

Much was made—everything was made—of my closeness to Ronald Reagan; that no matter what services I sold or how I labeled them, no client was likely to ignore the fact that he was hiring Reagan's "Friend."

They called it "access." I called it that myself, in conversations with reporters. It was one of the operative words in Washington. But I did not try to build a business on the fact that I worked for the president; nor did I feel I should be denied the right to start one for that reason.

Actually, no one ever accused me of breaking a law. It was the *appearance* of wrongdoing that brought forth so much righteous indignation. Said one congressman, Ron Wyden, a Democrat from Oregon: "My constituents are not asking about Section 207 [the conflict of interest provisions of the law]. They are saying, 'Is this really the normal way things are being done in Washington?'"

Yes, lawyers leave the White House staff and become partners in gargantuan law firms. Economists move to Wall Street for seven-figure salaries. Senators and congressmen become lobbyists for industries they once investigated. This news must be as shocking to Congressman Wyden as the discovery of another kind of conduct was for Captain Renault, in the movie *Casablanca,* when he gazed around Rick's Bar and said, "I am shocked—shocked!—to find that gambling is going on in here."

I can look back now and see that I was careless, stupid, inattentive to the enemies I had made. And greedy? So many people have written and said that I was, including some whose opinion I respect. (I am looking at a quote from a story in *The New Yorker:* "A prominent Washington attorney who has been on friendly terms with Deaver says, 'What amazes me is that Deaver has used such poor judgment. What happened to him clearly is that he'd never had any money in his life and he saw that he could make some and he went crazy. It happens with women, it happens with gambling, it happens with money.'") Maybe so. But greed didn't drive me.

I did not see myself as Daddy Warbucks; the idea for the company had modest beginnings. When one has to deal with the criminal-justice system, one needs a lawyer. When one deals with the federal government, one needs a road map to get through the maze. Our map was called strategic planning. I knew I could assemble a first-rate staff, and I did: Fred Hale, Bill Sittmann, Pam Bailey, others whose names would not be known to the public. But there was no assurance we could sell the services I felt we were equipped to provide.

When I left the White House I had no clients. One of the first

calls to come in was from a fellow who said he represented Carl
Icahn. He offered me, us, half a million dollars to represent
Icahn in his fight to acquire Trans World Airlines. I knew nothing about takeovers. I did not want to start off doing that kind
of short-term job. I thanked the caller for his interest and told
him it was out of our line.

But the call had started the wheels turning. It occurred to me
that if I could help TWA turn away Icahn's takeover attempt, I
could then provide TWA a wide range of services on a long-term
basis. I telephoned Jack Valenti, who had been on Lyndon
Johnson's staff in the mid-1960s and was on the board of TWA.
I told him why I was calling.

Valenti asked me to stay by the phone. Half an hour later, I
had a call from Ed Meyer, the president of the airline. He said
Valenti had told him about our company. He asked how much
we charged. Up to that moment, I had not been signatory to a
deal bigger than buying my own home. But I cleared my throat,
said that we planned to represent a limited number of clients
and our standard fee was $250,000.

Meyer said a check and an agreement would be on my desk in
a day or so.

I remember talking about our prospects with Fred Hale even
as the furniture was being moved into our offices. Hale, who
prided himself on his financial projections, said we would have
to put together $1 million in contracts by the end of the first year
to cover the line of credit borrowed to start the business.

By Christmas we had billed $4.5 million. The whole staff was
caught up in the euphoria of it. The volume of work was such
that we had no time, nor desire, to stop and analyze what we
were doing right.

Most of the first few clients were U.S.-based companies resist-
ing takeovers or involved in tax bills, among them Smith
Barney, TWA, and CBS. Then the foreign clients came in: Canada, companies from Saudi Arabia and South Korea (Daewoo
Steel). We were enjoying a success bigger than anything we had
dreamed, and yet we were pocket change next to the leaders in
the field. Gray and Company billed $28 million annually.

One of the biggest public-relations firms in the country, Burson-Marsteller, had offered me a salary in the $300,000 range to join its Washington office. My close friends had urged me to take it, pointing out that a year or two of institutional "cover" would be good for me. The money was more than I could expect to take out of my own company in the first year. But I wanted to run my own shop. And I wanted my own name out there.

Given my association with the president, I knew the first day we opened our doors that we would come under more than the normal scrutiny. I rewrote the book on image making, right? I thought I had bent over backward to keep ours clean. We paid for what I believed to be the best legal advice in town. We ran every proposal past our attorneys.

It is hard to capture the sheer pleasure of a place where an idea grows and comes to life before your eyes; where people, newly thrown together, come to work excited and stay late. We grew fast, but we came down faster. By the time our suppliers caught up with the orders for more phone lines and more desks, they were being disconnected and moved out.

We had been in business only a few months when the British company, Saatchi and Saatchi, offered to acquire us in a complicated transaction that could net us as much as $18 million over the next seven years. Among its clients, many of them international, S&S had at one point managed an image-enhancing campaign for Margaret Thatcher. We met in London and Washington, our top people and theirs. The contracts were drawn, ready to be signed. The merger meant that we would be able to test on a global scale the strategies that a short time earlier existed only on yellow scratch pads.

I could not resist calling Nancy and pouring out the details of this development. I felt like a fellow shot out of a cannon. But Nancy tried to bring me back to earth: "Mike, be careful," she urged. "I have a feeling this is all happening too fast."

What I had not done was step back and take a hard enough look at what people were saying and thinking, the public-relations problem I was creating.

I may be giving these rumblings a sharper edge than they

had. But there was a new battlefield in town, and I seemed
to be supplying all the soldiers and shedding all the blood.
The lobbyists—in whose ranks I still did not feel we belonged—
were wailing to reporters that my profile was too high. Stories
were popping into print: I was too eager to sign up too
many clients, made too much money too quickly and bragged
about it.

"Whether or not he actually broke the law," one article
would conclude, "he broke even the relatively relaxed norms
of behavior here. For this, he has been and will be pursued
and punished. Already, some clients are concluding that it is
poor public relations to have Deaver as a public-relations adviser."

And in *Time,* Hugh Sidey wrote: "Now comes Mike Deaver
with a new art form. He spent so many years in honorable service to a man (Reagan) and a cause (Republican conservatism)
that he could rightly claim some rewards. But once he headed
out of the White House and into the public-relations business,
all sense of proportion seemed to desert Deaver. The idea of
Deaver selling his year-old firm—founded almost exclusively on
his Reagan intimacy—for some $18 million would be perfectly
legal, and perfectly appalling."

As it happened, we killed the Saatchi and Saatchi deal after
protracted and increasingly unsatisfying negotiations. But it is a
painful and shrinking feeling to watch your judgment faulted,
especially by someone whose work you admired. When Sidey
accused me of using the president, I was devastated. That hit me
in a spot where I am vulnerable.

From the disclosure of the first investigation, Reagan had
stood by me. "Mike hasn't done anything wrong," he said.
"He has never put the arm on me." Nothing troubled me
more than having him put in a position where he felt he had to
defend me.

Actually, he seemed even more puzzled than I was by the
charges, and less inclined to accept the seriousness of them. On
one occasion, he showed that he had remembered well one of
my long-standing rules: that sometimes it helps to change the
subject.

Just about the time I was due to testify before the Oversight and Investigations Subcommittee of the House Energy and Commerce Committee, America's warplanes flew across the North Atlantic. A joking Reagan phoned and said, "Well, Mike, I bombed Libya for you."

A philosopher once said: "If you will not think me foolish because of my laughter, I will not think you wise because you frown." Many a time I had seen Ronald Reagan joke his way around a problem. But I was never one to take trouble lightly, and I believed in the theory that if things can get worse they always will.

For obvious reasons, I cut back my contacts with the White House, and kept my distance until Nancy called on me during the Iran-Contra uproar. To this day, the president has not asked me about, nor made any reference to, my business problems.

Unlike most other Washington hit-and-run casualties, I was aware of the actual source of the early criticism—the *Washington Times*.

A young man named George Archibald, a deputy assistant secretary in the U.S. Education Department, had been told to look for another job. His superiors disagreed with certain of his views. His name was then unknown to me, but the exit of anyone who styled himself a Reagan "purist" was often blamed on the attendant lords, the closet moderates, Deaver, Baker, or Richard Darman.

Archibald wound up as a national political reporter for the *Washington Times*. The South Korean cult leader, Sun Myung Moon, had founded the *Times* as an alternative to what he saw as the anti-Nixon bias of the media—and the country—after Watergate.

The conversation with Archibald, and a fellow reporter, was a rambling one, but loaded with questions carefully pointed. I felt they were based on gossip, and tissues of fact, that could have been dropped only by sources close to the new White House staff. My continuing relationship with the Reagans, to the point of being called in for occasional advice, was seen as an irritant there.

A month or so later, I was on vacation, in Antigua, when I accepted a call from a writer for *The Washington Post*. There was one phone available on my end of the island, and he had tracked down the number. He said, "I got a source that says you're being bought out by a Japanese advertising company."

His source must have thought the name was Saki and Saki. But his information was generally correct. The next week, an item about the offer from Saatchi and Saatchi appeared on the "Periscope" page of *Newsweek* (owned by the *Post*).

That rumor appeared on April 4, almost a month to the day after my picture ran on the cover of *Time* magazine. Next, a White House source leaked a story that I had met with James Miller, the director of the Office of Management and Budget, on behalf of Rockwell International, the contractor for the B-1 bomber—and suggested that I might thereby have violated the lobbying restrictions.

Acting on this lead, the General Accounting Office delivered a letter notifying me that it had been asked by a member of Congress to look into my activities. I called the person who signed the letter, and asked her to identify the congressman. She said she was not at liberty to say. I asked if she could tell me what had happened to my rights under the Constitution? She had no answer. I said, "Tell you what. Just call the congressman back and tell him I said he can take that letter and stick it . . ."

She called back later that day. "I told the congressman exactly what you said, and he said to tell you his name. It's John Dingell."

From a faceless cloud, the opposition was beginning to acquire names and shapes. Dingell was the powerful chairman of the House Energy and Commerce Committee. His district in Michigan produced more of the pollutants found in acid rain than any other area of the country. The next development found William Safire, a onetime Agnew and Nixon speechwriter turned *New York Times* columnist, calling for a special prosecutor. This has been a favorite tactic of Safire ever since he left the Nixon White House. By repeatedly calling for special prosecutors, and tagging every political controversy with the "gate" syllable, he attempts to inflate them to Watergate dimensions—a path that sometimes leads to a Pulitzer.

I find it particularly hard to shrug off the attacks of people like Bill Safire, political hatchetmen turned moralizers. By tackling a Republican target of lesser shading, they pay lip service to being objective.

Day after day I read the stories, the criticisms, saw myself painted as greedy or arrogant or with a certain contempt for civilized standards of conduct. I kept wondering what had happened, where had the train left the rails? Had I really miscalculated this badly? Had I ridden the wind and, in seven months, blown a reputation for integrity that had been twenty years in the making? To borrow a famous Watergate phrase, had I lost my moral compass?

But other questions troubled me as well: Who was my accuser? There was no Whittaker Chambers to be seen, making charges, spewing out testimony, directing the case. Exactly what had I done? The law prohibits an ex–federal employee from representing anyone before his former agency for one year after leaving the government, and from lobbying on any issue in which he "personally and substantially" participated.

My agency was the Oval Office. Not for one minute, nor one penny, did I lobby Ronald Reagan or anyone under him for special favors or courtesies. I reject any implication by the hypocrites and cheap-shot artists that I somehow paraded down Pennsylvania Avenue wearing a sandwich board advertising a presidential friendship for sale.

Then there is the finer point of whether I lobbied on an issue in which I may have influenced policy.

Acid rain.

I got involved in the subject of acid rain while the White House was preparing for a U.S.-Canadian summit meeting in 1985. I have noted one interesting coincidence: My pursuer in this matter was John Dingell, whose home state, Michigan, would bear new burdens under laws to reduce acid rain.

My efforts in connection with the summit had to do with public-relations-type issues, and had been directed at avoiding anything that might torpedo a meeting between Reagan and Canada's prime minister, Brian Mulroney. At that point, all I knew about acid rain was that you had smokestacks at one end (the United States) and dead fish at the other (Canada). All along, one curious aspect has been the fact that no one ever claimed I was on the wrong side of the issue; or that I made any recommendation that went against U.S. interests.

As it unfolded, the case against me was never as interesting as the coalition of people who brought the charges or pushed them along. When an officer of the General Accounting Office testified at the hearings that its original information had come from a White House staffer—that Deaver had cut a deal during the talks to work for the Canadians—a congressman asked which staffer.

When the witness said, "Stockman," the whole hearing room exploded in laughter.

David Stockman's motivation was no mystery to me. When the now famous interview with Stockman appeared in *The Atlantic,* labeling the Reagan economic plan a giant hoax on the American people, I wanted him fired on the spot. Instead, in what was reported to the press as a "trip to the woodshed," he met with the president and later softened his words and his stand. But there was no verbal paddling in any fictional woodshed. Reagan heard him out, with a graciousness the situation did not seem to demand. Stockman put on a show for the press but left, feeling he had gotten Reagan's attention.

Now, from his base on Wall Street, he attacks the president's economic policy as a disaster that will leave the country in more desperate straits at the end of the decade than when it began. In effect, Stockman misled the country, and was less than candid with his president, for three years. Now he is a millionaire, and if not a hero, at least something just as marketable: an authority.

I had a role in the firing of Richard Allen and James Watt, and the resignation of Bill Clark. I made too many enemies, including members of the management of the Moonie paper, the *Washington Times.* As the former White House Enforcer, the keeper of the moral code, I can hardly blame those who found in my difficulty a reason for gloating.

Had I still been working in the study next to the Oval Office, I would have fired myself as a liability to the president. Whatever anyone wrote or thought, I held myself to the same, or higher, standards as I did those who served the president.

I learned one day that one of my own top assistants, Joe Canzeri, had received a sweetheart loan from Laurence Rockefeller to finance a house. That very day I walked into his office and said, 'Joe, you have to go. You can stick around two months and fight it, and the White House can't do anything about it. But that will not help the president. That isn't why you came here, is it?"

Joe did not argue. He resigned, an act of grace. And no one was able to play politics with his case.

The difference was that I no longer worked at the White House. No one could fire me or accept my resignation. But the endless investigation, generating almost daily negative stories, had virtually the same effect. One by one I watched our clients not renew their contracts; others I released out of sympathy for the positions they were in. The Canadian government was one.

Some of my associates moved on to more secure jobs. And as the months went by with dwindling income, we kept reducing the secretarial and administrative staff. As the investigation dragged into a second year, we found smaller offices. Our payroll had been reduced from a high of twenty-one to less than half a dozen. My legal bills climbed past the half-million-dollar mark. I was, as a practical matter, broke. The euphoria of the first few months had vanished.

It was like watching somebody drown.

My eleven-year-old son, Blair, begged me to go to work before he left for school, so those in his sixth-grade car pool would not see him run the gauntlet of TV cameras and reporters out in front of our home. Carolyn complained of migraines. Old friends were not in when my calls came.

But encouragement came in from unexpected sources, too. Hamilton Jordan, who had been a target of the special prosecutor in the Carter administration, telephoned to say he knew what I was going through. So did Richard Helms, the former CIA director, who pleaded no contest to a perjury count in

1977. Bob Strauss, who came from the other side of the aisle,
kept taking me to breakfast.

How much of my problems were caused by "politics," and
how much by my failure to understand the morals of the mar-
ketplace, I cannot honestly say. Not yet. Perhaps by the end of
this marathon I will understand all too well.

As charges were dropped and replaced with new ones, as the
special prosecutor sought and won an indictment, as my lawyers
and his did their dance, I kept reading that it didn't matter
whether or not I traded on my "access" to Reagan. Everyone
knew the access was there.

Accusations of this kind are invaluable, since they have the
virtue of being almost impossible to answer.

I suppose what I resent most is listening to members of Congress tell me I had violated a public trust. At about the same
time they were criticizing me, several members of Dingell's subcommittee each accepted a thousand-dollar honorarium and
were treated to a VIP visit to a coal mine—by an industry they
regulate.

There is a saying in Washington that the left and the right
meet behind your back. The irony was never lost on me. I knew
that at least a part of my problems originated with the "Jim
Jones Wing" of the Republican party, those willing to prove
their loyalty by drinking the spiked Kool-Aid.

I did tend to feel surrounded, unsure where the larger threat
was coming from: the four Democrats on John Dingell's subcommittee? the news media? or my old antagonists on the far
right? I had undercut the Democrats somewhat by issuing my
own call for a special prosecutor, who turned out to be Whitney
North Seymour, Jr. As a Republican office seeker from New
York, he once lost a race to a candidate backed by Ronald
Reagan.

At times, if not for bad luck, I would have had no luck at all.

I thought I had friends among the press, and I did, although
they were not always the people I expected. Nicholas Von
Hoffman of *The Washington Post,* a columnist with liberal credentials, someone I hardly knew, called the case "deeply troubling" and taking on "an unpleasant odor. If Michael Deaver

has violated the lobbying laws, he should be prosecuted for violating the lobbying laws. What's this perjury stuff? It reeks of trickery, of prosecutors finding they don't have enough evidence to get the guy on a substantive charge but have found some cunning ways of phrasing the questions to catch this man by trapping him. . . ."

Do I feel singled out? At the risk of seeming petty, let me point out that on the same day the charges against me were disclosed, three members of the Walker family were arrested in a naval spy scandal that may have been the most harmful since the Rosenberg trial. My story stayed on the front page longer than theirs. Elsewhere, one reads that big banks launder Mafia money. Several marines in Moscow are charged with selling their honor for sex. Other spies sell out for spite and petty cash. A preacher sells out God for a quick thrill in a hotel room. American planes flying supplies to the Contras return with a cargo loaded with drugs.

If I do not misread the criticism against me, I might have avoided any problems had I chosen not to use the experience I had gained in twenty years as a state and federal employee. I find that oddly hypocritical, not unlike asking a pilot who retires from the air force not to seek a job with a commercial airline. What was I expected to do—brain surgery?

Nor do I feel I committed any wrong by representing clients, whether companies or foreign governments, that needed a presence in Washington.

On May 16, 1986, I testified before the House Subcomittee on Oversight and Investigations. I have here excerpted part of my testimony:

> One year and one week ago today, I left the White House and nearly twenty years of work for Ronald Reagan to begin a new chapter in my life. . . . I thought I was returning to private life. I realize now that once a high-level public servant, always a public figure. . . .
>
> I take very seriously the charges that have been leveled against me personally, against my firm, against my

profession and, by inference, against the president and the tradition of public service to which many of us have dedicated our lives. . . . I only ask not to be judged on the basis of anonymous leaks.

I'd like to start with some basics. What does my firm, Michael K. Deaver and Associates, do? To read news reports, one would think I am a one-man operation who takes big fees from clients for doing nothing more than placing phone calls and having meetings with top government officials.

Nothing could be farther from the truth. The services my firm provides to its clients are typical of those provided by most Washington-based consulting or public-relations firms—that is, we perform analyses of public issues to assist clients in establishing specific objectives, and then prepare strategies for accomplishing those objectives. . . .

I was sensitive in opening the firm to the fact that some people might try to hire me for a quick fix or for easy access to the White House. I therefore resolved that I would only enter into long-term contracts; I would not be a firefighter, available for hire on an hourly or daily basis.

Mr. Chairman [I am addressing John Dingell, here], as you know all too well yourself, the suggestion that I, or anyone in this town, could turn an issue around by a phone call to the president or to a Cabinet member does a disservice to our government. Patient, detailed, and substantive work that covers all segments of the policy process is the only way to succeed on an issue, and even then there is no guarantee of success.

In staffing the firm, I was careful to choose experts in the fields of communications, public affairs, economics, trade . . . my associates have served in four administrations, on both sides of the Hill, in the Departments of State, Energy, Transportation, the Federal Reserve Board, and in private industry. To suggest that all we have to offer a client are my personal contacts is an insult not only to my former colleagues in government, but to these fine people on my staff. . . .

On the matter of my firm's representation of foreign governments: All of [these] clients are strong allies of the United States and I would have it no other way. To the extent that friendly foreign governments are able to work smoothly and effectively in Washington, relations between the two nations can only be improved.

Third, the service I render to these foreign clients is the same as that performed on behalf of my domestic clients—the basis of which is *not* my relationship with the Reagans, but rather my firm's understanding of our economic and political system. . . .

Fourth, in representing my foreign clients—whether governmental or corporate—I have faithfully adhered to the Foreign Agents Registration Act. . . . In this regard, I note that some have criticized me on the ground that it is improper for any former presidential adviser ever to represent a foreign government in its dealings with [our own].

To these people I make the following response: Congress . . . fully considered the issue of the representation of foreign principals in the United States, particularly with respect to the possible impact on the national defense, internal security, and foreign relations. Despite numerous amendments to that act since it was first enacted sixty years ago, Congress never has even suggested the impropriety . . . these critics now assert. This law covers me and every other citizen—including former members of Congress—who may represent a foreign government. . . .

I have never traded on my relationship with the president for any client—and I never will. For four and a half years in the White House, and for fifteen before that, my total commitment—sometimes, I fear, to the detriment of my family—had been to serve Ronald Reagan and his best interests. I believe I have done that. . . .

The suggestion that after twenty years of selfless service I would suddenly begin to use that relationship for personal gain is not only mean-spirited, but is also an implicit attack on the integrity of the president."

The investigation started by the GAO was joined by two congressional committees, the Office of Government Ethics, and the special prosecutor's office. The allegations, when you cut out the legalspeak, boiled down to influence peddling. I was accused of using my former White House contacts on behalf of a variety of clients. No matter how my actions were twisted or stretched, weighed or analyzed, I was not guilty of those charges.

The investigators conceded as much when they were unable to build the case they had sought. Instead, I was indicted on five counts of perjury. In Washington, if they can't get you on anything else, they will usually take a stab at perjury.

If in the end I have failed to convince a jury of my innocence, then it will mean nothing if I win the case in my own book. So I struggle to see things clearly. I voluntarily testified on two separate occasions for a total of about eleven and a half hours and answered truthfully well more than a thousand questions. Contradictions were found in five of my answers, most of which consisted of a failure to recall details the prosecutor says I must have recalled. I realize that the legal system does not grade us on a curve. But no matter how often I reread the transcripts, or hear the words echo in my mind, they do not seem as sinister to me as they clearly did to the special prosecutor.

The first two counts against me were related to my testimony before the Subcommittee on Oversight and Investigations. In brief, I was accused of lying to conceal a telephone call I am alleged to have made to a former associate at another agency— the National Security Council—on behalf of a client, the government of South Korea. No one argued, by the way, that this was other than a clearly permissible contact.

The excerpts that follow are taken directly from the grand jury indictment. During this portion of the hearings, which began on May 16, 1986, I was being questioned by Mark Raabe, a subcommittee staff counsel:

Q. And what was the subject of that contact?

A. The subject, the content of that subject, was to find out from an informational standpoint if Mr. Kim Kihwan, representing the president of Korea, had an appointment with the president.

Q. You checked with Mr. Martin [William Martin, of the National Security Council] to see whether Mr. Kim Kihwan had an appointment with the president. And when was that?

A. I don't have the date. I am sorry.

Q. I believe your counsel has it.

A. That would have been October first, 1985.

Q. And what was the result of your inquiry of Mr. Martin?

A. I am not certain. I think that Mr. Martin told him that that had been a request from the Korean Ambassador, and was in the process.

Q. You are saying that Mr. Sittmann checked with Mr. Martin?

A. Yes, sir.

Q. And it was in process?

A. The request was in process already through normal diplomatic channels.

Q. The request from whom?

A. The request from the Korean government.

Q. Did you do anything to facilitate that request?

A. No, sir.

Q. You did not contact anyone further than the contact with Mr. Sittmann to Mr. Martin?

A. No, sir.

The indictment charged that the underscored answers were false because I had allegedly suggested to the South Koreans that they send an emissary to deliver a personal letter, concerning trade issues, from their president to President Reagan and allegedly had contacted Richard Walker, our ambassador to South Korea, and John Poindexter, at the National Security Council, to arrange the meeting.

The meeting, which essentially consisted of a photo opportunity, did take place in October 1985, and lasted a total of two minutes. The South Korean government was not yet a client of my firm.

The second count of perjury alleged other executive-office contacts and stemmed from the following testimony:

Q. Let's go on to the next occasion that you consulted with your counsel, prior to contacting someone within the center of the White House.
A. I don't recall any other occasion.
Q. Well, you don't recall. You don't recall. But you seem to recall six.
A. No. You asked me how many, and I said it could have been up to six.
Q. And you have now related one.
A. No. I think I have related two, haven't I? I related Mr. Miller [Budget Director James Miller].
Q. I beg your pardon. You have related two.
   Would it be helpful to search your memory further?
A. Those are the only two that I can recall. Once we had established that we could deal with certain members of the NSC and certain members of the OMB, we didn't check any further on those areas, and I didn't ever talk to anybody in the West Wing of the White House.
Q. Who else have you or your firm contacted at OMB on any matter?
A. I haven't contacted anybody at OMB.
Q. How about your firm? Your memory was just refreshed from behind you there [referring to one of my associates] and I thought . . .
A. He didn't talk to me about anybody else. I don't recall any other contacts with OMB.
Q. How about with NSC?
A. No, I don't recall any other contacts with NSC.
Q. But is it your testimony that there weren't additional contacts?

A. To the best of my knowledge, there weren't any other contacts, yes, sir.

The special prosecutor turned up seven contacts that I had with individuals who were either in the West Wing or at the National Security Council, one of whom was William Martin, about whom I had already testified—the assumption being that they were on behalf of various clients. His information may have been better than my memory, but I answered as openly as I could, without the opportunity to respond to specific names and references.

In counts three through five, I was accused of making false statements to a grand jury about my involvement with Trans World Airlines, the acid-rain issue, and Puerto Rico. The "TWA count" arose from the following testimony:

Q. Now let's turn to the actual development of the business, and do understand that for now at least, I'm still trying to develop the background of how your business operates. If at any point you think that I'm getting into areas that you have some reservation about answering, feel free to consult Mr. Miller [Herbert J. Miller and Randall J. Turk were my trial attorneys.]

Do you recall who the first bit of business that you had came from? Who was your first client?

A. I believe the first client I got was TWA.

Q. Do you recall how that happened, when it happened?

A. Yes. It happened on Memorial Day weekend, 1985. I got a call from—there was if you recall, and I'm sure you do, a takeover attempt of TWA. I got a call from a party who said that the people who were trying to take over TWA would like to hire me.

I decided I didn't want to do that as a first client, so I called a friend on the TWA board and said, "Look, I don't want to do this. It's not the kind of business that I want to get into, but I would like to work for TWA if they would be interested in hiring me, the current ownership, but I would only want to do it on an annual contract. If I could do the kinds of things that I want to do in strategic planning for TWA, I would be happy to work on the takeover, too, but I want to do other things."

So they agreed—TWA agreed to hire me.

Q. And were there strategic-planning needs that you were already aware of when you contacted your friend?

A. No, but I would assume that any major corporation had a need for strategic planning.

Q. So at that time you didn't know specifically what you were going to do for them?

A. No, I did not.

Q. Eventually, did any of the work you did for that client involve business with government agencies or at least involving you personally? I'm not talking about routine, regulatory—

A. I'm sorry?

Q. Did any of your work for TWA involve personal contact by you as opposed to staff people with government officials?

A. I don't recall any government contact I made on behalf of TWA.

The indictment charged that the underscored answer was false because I allegedly had made three calls on behalf of TWA: one to Elizabeth Dole, the secretary of transportation; one to her deputy; and one to the Cabinet Council on Economic Policy. None of the calls was noteworthy, none required action—by them or by me—and none was illegal. Why would I deliberately try to conceal them?

The most serious count against me related to whether I had "substantial" discussions with the Canadian representatives regarding the acid-rain problem. This was the first charge raised against me in public, and implied most strongly a misuse of my relationship to Ronald Reagan. Count four was the result of the following testimony:

Q. All right. Now let's get to acid rain. Would you tell us what your first recollection is of being present at any meeting while you were working in the White House where the subject of acid rain and relations with the government of Canada came up?

A. I don't recall any specific time, any specific reference to acid rain until we began the preparations for the summit in March.

Q. March of 1985?

A. March of 1985. What might be the easiest thing for me would be to go through a chronology of meetings that I had and tell you if the subject of acid rain came up at that time.

Q. This is something that you prepared for your appearance today?

A. Yes, sir.

Q. Go right ahead.

A. On December eleventh, 1984, Canadian Ambassador [Allan] Gotlieb and Mr. Fred Doucet, from the prime minister's office, came to Washington to meet with various government officials to plan the meeting between the president and the prime minister on March the seventeeth in Quebec.

During that visit they stopped by my office and we talked largely about the kinds of requirements the president would need on that visit, set a date for me bringing an advance team up to Quebec, and I told them the kinds of people I would be bringing so that he could have counterparts there. I don't recall the subject of acid rain specifically coming up at that meeting.

On December the seventeenth, 1984, I took our advance team to Quebec and met during that day with the Canadian team. Along with the people that I described before, the military people, the security people, the medical people, the advance people, the press people that I would normally take, we took along some substantive people from the National Security Council, and I believe someone from the State Department. The person from the National Security Council was Mr. Ty Cobb.

That day was largely a planning—it started off with a planning meeting when we arrived in Quebec. We then spent most of the morning visiting various sites that the Canadians were suggesting for the different venues that would be going on during the summit.

We came back, had a working lunch, and then the people who were involved in the actual logistical advance went off and we looked at other sites.

The substantive people then met with the substantive people from the Canadian government. I don't recall at any time being involved in any conversation on acid rain during that visit.

[Editorial aside: As I reread these words now, I am not certain how much light this exchange may shed on the case against me, or on how the country is run. But it does show how one can get caught up in the bureaucratic language. I thought I was immune to it.]

Q. Did you join either group?
A. Yes. I went with the advance logistical people.

On February twenty-eighth, 1985, Mr. Doucet stopped by my office and he was in town, in Washington, D.C., doing a follow-up for the summit, and I briefly talked to him about the preparations. Again I do not recall the subject of acid rain coming up.

On March sixth, 1985, we had a meeting of the summit planning group, the American team. This was not the team that I described as an advance team. This was, I believe, Mr. [Robert] McFarlane, the secretary of state [George Shultz], Mr. Ty Cobb, Mr. Dave Stockman, Mr. Jack Svahn from the White House Office of Policy Development, myself, and there may have been two or three other people from the NSC or the State Department.

It was at that time—let me go back. On any summit

meeting, economic summit, or bilateral summit, or major trip of the president, we had developed a system where the national security adviser and myself co-chaired a summit planning group, so that's why I would be at this meeting.

There was a brief discussion of the logistics for the summit and then began a discussion of the agenda for the meeting. The subject of acid rain came up and the State Department and the National Security Council were very concerned that the subject of acid rain was going to ruin the summit. It was, as they described, a primary political problem in Canada and they felt it was important for the United States, and particularly the president, to indicate some concern. He could not simply go to Canada and brush off the subject of acid rain.

I believe also that [Richard] Burt was at that meeting. It was either Rick Burt or Bud McFarlane who, I believe, broached the idea of the appointment of a special envoy, that the United States would appoint a special envoy and the Canadian government would appoint a special envoy to study the issue of acid rain as it affected our two countries.

David Stockman, and I believe Jack Svahn, argued strongly against the appointment of a special envoy. Mr. Stockman had argued that he had just recently been successful in getting a decision against Mr. [William] Ruckelshaus to develop a major approach to the acid-rain problem in a Cabinet meeting because of the costs, and that the appointment of a special envoy would simply open up, I think as he called it, Pandora's box.

I spoke out in favor of the special envoy, and I spoke out largely for political reasons. It seemed to me to be a reasonable and easy way for the president to get by the summit without having a major negative issue develop.

There was no decision made at that meeting.

On March twelfth, 1985, Ambassador Gotlieb came

by my office and talked to me about the plans for the
summit. He told me that the special-envoy idea was
still being discussed. He didn't ask for anything from
me and I didn't offer anything.

On March thirteenth, there was a senior staff meeting, the eight o'clock meeting in the Roosevelt Room.
One of the items was the summit and the appointment
of a special envoy on acid rain. I don't recall participat-
ing in that discussion but I remember the discussion.

Sometime between March the thirteenth and March
the seventeenth, Bud McFarlane or Ty Cobb, I can't
remember which, either stopped me in the hall or
dropped by my office to tell me that the special-envoy
idea was moving forward and that they were going to
recommend two—they had two possible candidates.
One was William Clark, the former national security
adviser, and the other was Drew Lewis, the former secretary of transportation.

They asked me what I thought about that and I said
that either of those would be fine, perfectly acceptable
to me. On March the seventeenth, we went to Quebec
to the summit. I did not participate in any meetings of
the summit.

That's the chronology of the meetings that I can recall having to do with acid rain.

Q. Let me make sure that I understand what you said
about when you first participated in any meeting in
which there was a discussion of the subject. If I followed you correctly, it was the March sixth, 1985—that
was the first time that the subject of acid rain was ever
discussed in your presence as far as you recall?

A. Well, acid rain was a subject that had been discussed
at previous meetings with Canadians, but it was not a
subject I participated in. As far as this particular summit was concerned, that is the first time that I can recall.

Q. Tell us a little bit more about what the earlier discussions were.

A. I don't recall.

Q. I'm only talking about ones where you were yourself present.

A. I don't recall frankly any other meetings where the subject of acid rain came up that I participated in. Acid rain as an issue between the Canadian government and the United States government was always, I believe, since we have been in the White House, on the agenda for any bilateral meetings since it was a tremendous political issue in Canada.

I don't recall my specific participation in any discussion on acid rain until the meeting on March the sixth.

Q. How about the subject of special envoy or special ambassador? Do I also understand that that subject first came to your attention on March the sixth 1985?

A. To the best of my recollection that is the first time that I heard the concept of special envoy.

Q. And I assume that you have spent some time searching your recollection on this subject?

A. Yes, sir. . . .

*   *   *

Q. And it is your recollection that when Ambassador Gotlieb—I'm not sure we've identified him yet. He's the Canadian ambassador to the United States?

A. Yes.

Q. Spelled G-o-t-l-i-e-b?

A. Right.

Q. When he and Mr. Doucet came to meet you at the White House, it is your recollection that they did not raise the question of acid rain at any point in that meeting with you?

A. They could have. I don't recall it.

Q. How about the subject of the special envoy?

A. I don't recall that. The first I recall the special envoy is on March the sixth.

Q. Do you recall having lunch with Ambassador Gotlieb at any time during this period?

A. No, sir.

Q. Do you recall having lunch with Ambassador Gotlieb in January of 1985?

A. No, sir. I was in the hospital in January of 1985 for ten days and I was also chairman of the Inaugural so I was pretty busy, but I don't recall any such lunch.

Q. Do you recall any luncheon meeting with Ambassador Gotlieb at any time during this period?

A. No, I do not and I have checked all my schedules.

Q. Do you recall ever indicating to Ambassador Gotlieb that you had discussed the question of a special envoy with Secretary Shultz and that he had no objection to the idea?

A. No, sir.

Q. How did the—I beg your pardon. I've got one other meeting to ask you about.

Do you recall a meeting on January the thirty-first, 1985, with Mr. Doucet to discuss the subject of the special envoy?

A. January thirty-first?

Q. 1985.

A. I wasn't even in the White House. I was either in the hospital or just getting out.

Q. You were not in the office at all on that day?

A. Not according to my schedule.

Q. During what time were you in Europe?

A. February fifteenth through February twenty-eighth.

Q. So that your meeting with Mr. Doucet on the twenty-eighth was your first day back in the office?

A. Yes, sir. I had no scheduled appointments on that day. I just had come back from the hospital.

Q. Was he the only appointment you had on that day?

A. No. Obviously, when I got into the office I saw other people, but I had no scheduled appointments. He was not scheduled. He just dropped in.

Q. And it is your present recollection that neither the

subject of acid rain nor the subject of the special envoy was raised by Mr. Doucet in that face to face meeting with you?

A. That is my recollection, yes.

*   *   *

Q. Do you recall attending a meeting on March the second, 1985, of a working group to plan the Canadian trip that included Mr. Regan, Mr. McFarlane, and yourself?

A. No, sir, I don't.

Q. Can you look at your notes and see if you did attend such a meeting?

A. I have been asked that question before the Dingell committee, too, and I do not—it is not on my schedule and I do not recall the meeting.

*   *   *

Q. Did you yourself take any role in actually selecting the person who became the envoy, that is, Mr. Lewis?

A. No, sir.

Q. Did you speak to Mr. Lewis about doing it?

A. No, I did not.

Q. Do you know how the two candidates, Mr. Clark and Mr. Lewis, were chosen between? Did the president himself make the choice?

A. I assume he did. I'm sure he did.

Q. Did you consult with him about that?

A. No, sir, I did not.

Q. Do you know who did?

A. No, I don't. I mean, I don't have a recollection. I would assume that that occurred with a meeting with the secretary and Mr. McFarlane.

Q. But you yourself had no part in that?

A. No, sir.

Q. Did you have any conversation with Mr. Lewis prior

to the public announcement of his appointment about
his becoming special envoy?
A. <u>No, sir.</u>
Q. You're quite clear about that?
A. <u>To the best of my recollection. I cannot recall hav-
ing any conversation with Mr. Lewis about that.</u>

The indictment listed six meetings—three of which I testified
to having attended—at which "the acid-rain question" allegedly
was discussed. In addition, I was said to have supported the idea
of a special envoy from the start, and to have supported and
spoken to Drew Lewis on the day the president asked him to
serve.

Since none of these actions was illegal or even in bad form, I
can think of no reason why I would not have disclosed them if
they had happened the way the special prosecutor suggested
they had, and I had remembered them. You can be made to
look foolish or evasive by repeating that you do not remember.
But sometimes there is no mystery. You just don't remember.

The implication was that I had taken the Canadian position on
acid rain in order to obtain their account later for my company.
The legal nuances probably escape me, but there was nothing
complex about Canada's position on acid rain. They were
against it. So were we. The question was what should be done.
When we named a special envoy to talk about it everyone
yawned. It was not exactly like sending in the fleet.

But that bone was one the investigators never tired of chewing
on. When I appeared before the Subcommittee on Oversight
and Investigations, their counsel, Patrick McLain, informed me
that Bud McFarlane, and others, had given statements that I
had attended senior staff meetings, that I had participated in
discussions, and that acid rain had been mentioned there:

Q. Are you testifying that these people did not testify
truthfully?
A. I have given you, to the best of my knowledge, a list
of any meetings I attended regarding acid rain or the
appointment of a special envoy.

No one asked Bud McFarlane, or any other witnesses, if I was still in the room—if and when that subject actually came up. How long I stayed sometimes depended on how long it took to call the roll.

That answer may seem flippant or indifferent. I have not taken these charges, or at least their consequences, lightly. But what I found maddening was the repetition of the questions, as if I was on trial for forgetting a lunch or a meeting. I did not merely attend a thousand meetings. I attended the same meeting a thousand times.

I had as much right to interpret the facts as the prosecution did, but with one difference. Their way could lead to prison. I thought of that when certain material from the subcommittee hearings found its way into the first and second counts. What the special prosecutor labeled as untruths struck me as legal hairsplitting.

The fifth and last count had to do with the effort of Puerto Rico to obtain tax relief, under Section 936 of the Internal Revenue code. We were brought in as a consultant by the investment bankers, Smith Barney Harris Upham & Co. One sentence was cited in my testimony:

> Q. Did you yourself have any contacts or conversations relating to the 936 issue with anybody in the federal government apart from Secretary [James] Baker.
> A. Secretary Baker and the people in the Treasury that I described?
> Q. Yes.
> A. I don't recall any such discussions.

Here the lines were more finely drawn. According to the indictment I had had conversations with three people with whom I worked at the White House: George Shultz, Craig Fuller, and Bud McFarlane. Seymour saw them as contacts.

I bumped into Shultz one afternoon and we joked about being on the same side of the 936 issue—it must have sounded like cop talk. I don't remember having made any calls to either Fuller, the vice-president's chief of staff, or McFarlane. Fuller doesn't recall that I called either. McFarlane recalls nothing more than a social call.

There is simply no way to answer the charges, except to say no, without seeming to cop a lesser plea. Of course, I am guilty of being careless about appearances. It was generally known at the time of the acid-rain talks that I would be leaving the White House. Four months after I opened my offices, we signed a contract as consultants to the Canadian government. The fee was $105,000.

The objective in part was to persuade the United States to clean up the acid rain that kept drifting across our northern border, polluting lakes, killing fish, and damaging timber. We developed a strategy, worked with environmental groups in both countries. But not once did I pursue the matter with the president nor, I repeat, with anyone with whom I had worked in the White House. Canada may feel it should have gotten more access than it did. After two years, there is still no agreement between the countries on this issue.

In reviewing my case, I have tried to exercise restraint, knowing that what I have said here will not determine the verdict. My fate ultimately rests with a jury. I believe I am innocent of the charges, and innocent of all the accusations save that of being the president's friend. But should I lose, there is not much else that can be taken away. I have had my business stripped from me, peeled off like a layer of skin. The money, the clients, the pretty good name, all are gone.

On a clear spring day in 1987, I met two reporters from *Newsweek* for an interview. They were friendly, the story mixed but not unfair. At one point they asked if I planned to keep the Jaguar XJ6. With a grin, I told them I did, and they quoted me verbatim:

"I figured, screw you guys. I love that car."

That turned out to be wishful thinking on my part. A few months later, the Jag was gone, too.

Out of the Mouths . . .

Our daughter, Amanda, grew up as a toddler knowing that I worked for the governor and he was in a position of authority. When Richard Nixon gave his speech in the East Room of the White House in August 1973, resigning the presidency, Amanda watched as her mother wept in front of the television set.

When Amanda asked her why she was crying, all Carolyn could think to say was "Because he lied."

How do you explain to a three-year-old that a man has violated his oath of office, and for the first time in the history of this country the man elected to its highest office has been forced to resign in shame?

The next time Carolyn brought Amanda to the governor's office, a few days later, she ran to Governor Reagan. He scooped her up and to everyone's surprise she began to cry. Reagan took her into his office and closed the door behind him. Carolyn and I just stared at each other.

Five minutes later, she walked out with a handful of jelly beans and her eyes dried.

As Amanda left with her mother, I asked Reagan, "What was that all about?"

"Beats me," he said, with a shrug. "She just kept asking me, 'You'll never lie, will you?'"

12
One Day
at
a Time

In a town not famous for keeping a secret, I kept one for years: covering most of my last twelve months at the White House, including the Bitburg crisis, through the giddy rise and slow strangulation of my own company, and the investigation of my activities by Congress and a special prosecutor.

The secret was of a personal kind, much less difficult to keep than to admit, one that brought me despair and pain and guilt. For the entire month of November 1986, I disappeared. Yet outside of my family and doctor, no one knew where I had gone. Until I told them, no one guessed the truth: not the Reagans, nor close friends, nor any member of my office staff.

I am an alcoholic.

I do not say those words for dramatic effect. Nor am I at all sure that they still retain any. We live in an age of substance abuse. Chemical dependence is so common among sports figures and entertainers that with each new disclosure, each new admission to the drug farm, the public reacts with less surprise. Boredom has begun to settle in.

This is no plea for sympathy, nor even for understanding. In the end, the one who needed to understand was me. This is where it begins for an addicted person. I have begun to come to terms with it: with the harm I did my family, with the constant fear I felt of being discovered and embarrassing the president, and finally, the pride I had to choke down to admit I was:

An alcoholic.

If my case is different in any way, it is only because I sat for many years at the right hand of the president. And for at least the last of those years, I had a serious drinking problem. How serious?

Let me make it clear: Life at times can be mean and unjust. Three out of three people will not leave this world alive, and it does little good to rail against the odds or the hard times. Most just get on with it. I do not blame my problems on the pressures of a job I loved, or the excitement of starting a new career, or the public flogging I felt was undeserved.

Overconfidence did me in. I read about my slick and astute self in the national press, Macho Mike and Mike the Magician, and I began to believe I could handle anything. It was not an illness that crept up on me unawares. It just crept.

Drinking to me always had been casual, a form of release and relaxation. That was how I saw it when the occasional drink made the night a little lighter on the piano-and-lounge circuit during my college days.

I still viewed myself as a social drinker in the early years of the Reagan administration. Then, one day, it began to dawn on me. I knew my body was demanding more and more. I would wake up in the morning and the only thing I thought about was how soon I would get to the liquor supply and where I would hide the bottle. It was a brutal feeling, this sense that if I didn't get a drink I would absolutely explode. With it, in waves, came the guilt of having to hide that part of my life, and then realizing that alcohol was now the principal priority in this secret life I led.

When I was honest with myself—not an easy or frequent condition—I was filled with self-contempt; not because of what I might be doing to my wife or the Reagans, but because the one thing I could never tolerate in myself was lack of control. To me, control was a measure of my character, my will, my worthiness. I had controlled my environment, my job, my family, my music, my tennis, all my relationships . . . but this, the one with the bottle, I could not control.

I drank to get me through the uproar over Bitburg, and to quiet the butterflies I felt over leaving the Reagans and starting out on my own without a client or a dime of investment capital. It was a scary time for me. I was physically exhausted, driving myself, shuttling back and forth to Europe and Asia. A lot of bills were coming due at once.

I had drawn pleasure from drinking—right up until the moment the next glass became a necessity. Then it was no longer a pacifier, or an emotional lift, or a quick buzz. I realized I needed it.

In early 1985, it began to sink in that I had a problem, but I was convinced I could cure myself. Later I checked into Georgetown Hospital, quietly, stayed three or four days, dried out, and felt like I had it under control until about nine months later when the investigation into my company picked up steam.

I had terrific mood swings and bouts of depression. At first, at the office, I tried to see how far into the day I could last before I took my first drink. I had one at lunch to calm me down. Lunch became a goal, and then it became Mount Everest. I was drinking almost as soon as I came through the door. Bottles were hidden in creative places . . . under desks or inside lamps. It was almost classic stuff, Ray Milland in *The Lost Weekend,* and painful though it is to recall now, I welcome the reminder of how miserable the disease really is.

The people who saw me every day, Carolyn at home, my brother, Bill, and Bill Sittmann and Fred Hale around the office, knew something was wrong. But if I seemed different, edgier, moody, why not? The strains were obvious. Only Hale came right out one day and asked me if I had been drinking. I said yes. He nodded and said no more. He had no idea how much.

In a tiny corner of my brain, I was proud of my deception, my secret. There was little to give me away: I did not humiliate myself at parties, did not get arrested for driving while intoxicated, did not jump into the Tidal Basin with a stripper or make love to my wife—or anyone else's wife—on the steps of Congress.

But, clearly, I was heading for a disaster. I could not have dreamed that when the showdown came, and with it the exposure I dreaded, the liberation I needed, who the central character would be.

Carolyn had gone to California for a college reunion, with my encouragment. I knew she needed to get away. It was getting to her, the daily stories, watching the business founder. I had been drinking steadily, privately, what I referred to as "maintenance" drinking, just to keep the engine running. That weekend I never stopped. I don't know how many bottles I emptied.

When Monday rolled around, I didn't feel like fighting it out at the office, meeting with the lawyers. So I called in, said I wasn't feeling well. I repeated myself on Tuesday.

That night, Amanda, my sixteen-year old daughter, walked into my study and asked what was wrong. I said, "It's nothing, I just have a touch of the flu."

She stood in the doorway and stared at me. "No, you don't," she said, and she spun around, went upstairs to her room, and called our doctor.

He was at the house in less than an hour. He knew of my earlier stay at Georgetown, my attempt to lick the problem more or less alone. I had only deluded myself. The doctor convinced me I should commit myself into an intensive program. "Mike, you can't handle this yourself. We must get you into a facility with professionals who will help you work it out." I checked into Georgetown Hospital that evening to begin detoxification.

The next day, Wednesday, I checked into the Ashley Center for Alcohol and Drug Rehabilitation in Havre de Grace, Maryland. The facility is run by a priest, Father Martin, who told me he had once stayed drunk off and on for twenty-six years.

At that point, fewer than half a dozen people knew my whereabouts. As far as anyone else was concerned, I had just dropped out of sight. Carolyn told them I was traveling.

I had been there ten days before Carolyn was permitted to visit me. We held each other for a long time, and kissed, and her cheeks were wet. When we finally got around to making human noises, she said, "Mike, Nancy [Reagan] has been calling every day. She is just beside herself, wanting to know where you are, how long you'll be gone, what you're doing."

I said, "It's okay. I'll call her tonight." Later, I asked if I could borrow a private office and I placed a call to the White House. When Nancy came on the line, she said, "My God, where are you?"

The words did not exactly dance off my tongue: "I'm at a place in Maryland where I'm getting some help . . . because I am an alcoholic."

"Thank God!" she said, forcefully. "Thank God, that's what it is."

I said, "Nancy, what are you saying? I just told you I'm an alcoholic. It's a terrible thing."

Calmly, she said: "No, it's a disease, and one you can handle. I was worried sick you might have cancer. This one you can cure."

For many of the twenty-eight days I underwent treatment at Ashley, I was paranoid, sure that every new patient was an undercover reporter for *The New York Times*. It was three weeks before I could stand up in an auditorium, identify myself, and tell my story. That was a turning point for me.

At Ashley, I found people who had been in situations similar to mine. The disease has no prejudices. It is a great equalizer, whether you are in the public eye or not. The fears and emotional problems are pretty much the same. I met people who became sources of strength to me, some who had been in government and others who were simply trying to cope with life in a private way.

Father Martin won my everlasting respect with his patience, his gentle concern. There are more delicate ways of saying this, but the way I felt then was lower than squid shit. (If my editor prefers a blank space to my language, you will know she bleeped me out.) Yet Father Martin never failed during the day to seek me out and tell me how much I was loved. You might be surprised how badly a grown person needs to hear that, even one who thinks he has acquired a layer of cynicism. I considered myself a religious person, who had once planned on entering the ministry. But Father Martin brought me to the first real understanding of my God, just by talking with me. I went to mass every morning I was there, and the service took on a new meaning for me. Praying with other alcoholics, and an alcoholic priest, gave me a sense of God's love I had never known.

All those funny little homilies I had heard for so long, such as taking life one day at a time, all acquired new meanings for me. They really do have relevance. One woman told me about a saying they had in her home for years, embroidered on a pillow: *"Fear knocked on the door, hope rose to answer and no one was there."* Trite, but also true. For the first time, I was able to accept the idea that we are voyagers in this life, and not everything is within our control.

I will pursue this theme no further. I have said what I needed to say. There is a risk of reinforcing the view that Washington officials, once in trouble, find it convenient to discover God in their hall closet.

The day after my return from the center, I went into my office and called a meeting of the entire staff. As deliberately as I could, I told them where I had been, and why, and how I was trying to deal with it. One by one, they gave me a hug and went back to work.

I knew I had a great deal to prove to my wife, who had endured the brunt of my mood changes, and who was frankly dubious that my stay at Ashley would produce the long-term changes that were needed. I have been sober since the day I got there. I no longer want a drink. I am not sure my body can stand one. Carolyn believes in me again, I hope. Alcoholism *is* permanent. It does not have to be terminal.

In some ways my biggest hurdle was to see the president, knowing Ronald Reagan's sensitivity to the drinking problem of his father. Jack Reagan had been a binge drinker. The president told me one time of a Christmas when his father passed out on the porch in the snow, and he and his brother, Neil, and their mother had dragged him into the house and put him to bed.

His mother called both boys aside and said, "Don't blame

your father. It's a disease." Keep in mind that we are talking about an incident that happened sixty years ago. That was a fairly enlightened lady for the times.

When I saw him, the president gave me a long, inquiring look, and touched my arm awkwardly. "My God, Mike," he said, "all the times we talked about my dad, and I never dreamed that you had a problem."

"Well, I did," I said. "Still do. But I'm getting a grip on it."

We did not directly address the subject again. But several days passed before he could bring himself to tell me another Irish drinking joke.

Nancy called every day. She wanted to know how I was doing, how my spirits were. She ended every conversation by saying, "I love you."

It was not without second and third thoughts that I elected to include in these pages an account of my personal demons. We would all like to say, like to feel, that we have done so for noble reasons, to help others who may be lost or troubled. My choice was not so clear. The lessons I learned, and the help I accepted, would seem invalid if I failed to maintain my sobriety. Nor, in defending against the charges brought by the special prosecutor, did I want to appear to be hiding behind my drinking, the confusion of that time, the absent days in Georgetown and Ashley.

I would have preferred that my condition, and my treatment, be kept private. But the reader is owed, I think, an acknowledgment that, one way or another, few of us will get out unmarked after twenty years in politics, at or near the center of power. What I will not offer up are the names, and privacy, of others with similar problems. One night, quite by accident, four of us spotted each other in a parking lot after a meeting on temperance. The others were a senator, a lobbyist, a former congressman.

Most of the reaction I have received has been somewhat more enlightened. I am friendly again with a fellow who had become a political foe, who overcame his own drinking problem. A clerk in a congressman's office, who is under thirty, and who sought help after his fiancée left him, walked up one day and said he admired me. I don't why. He just did.

I could with very little imagination go on for pages on how one comes to such a crossroads. It would be hard to spend four and a half years in the White House and emerge unspoiled. You are fawned over, and even granted a bit of an aura. The president has trusted you with a fair amount of responsibility; he does not tell you how to load the truck, he just wants it loaded.

After which, you pass through the looking glass and one of the largest companies in the world wants to talk to you about buying you out for millions of dollars. And the next moment you have been discredited by the press, and almost lost your business. Your family is shell-shocked. For the first time in years, you are forced to look at yourself, and where you are, and what you really want.

I realize now that I may have to start all over again. And yet, because my sixteen-year-old daughter had the courage to tell her father he was a drunk, I am not driven by the pressure of making money, or acquiring power, fame, or access.

I am at peace with myself, to the point that I paid a visit to Bud McFarlane in his hospital room three days after he tried to take his own life, in February 1987. No one had hailed McFarlane as a hero in the wake of the Iran-Contra scandal. But he had talked to the investigators, while others were taking the Fifth Amendment.

I told him what I had been through, how low I thought I had fallen, how I shared moments as dark as his. The only difference was that I reached for a bottle of booze, and he opened a bottle of Valium.

As we talked, I grew more aware of how similar our backgrounds were. We both had felt the same commitment and sense of duty to this president and, because of the circumstances, both of us felt we had failed.

His room was cluttered with flowers and boxes of candy, and one sympathetic stranger had mailed a videotape of the classic Frank Capra movie *It's a Wonderful Life,* starring Jimmy Stewart. Bud and his wife, Jonda, had watched it together in his

room. In the film, an angel saves Stewart from killing himself
and shows him how his town, and his friends, would have been
worse off if he had never lived.

McFarlane has said that his sense of failure was behind his
suicide attempt. He spoke of the president who did not "easily
absorb what he was told about foreign affairs," and who felt
more comfortable in the company of advisers who were self-
made and wealthy, as McFarlane was not. As I was not.

Reagan, he said, "admires men who have . . . demonstrated
considerable accomplishments in a chosen field. I haven't done
that. I had a career in the bureaucracy. It didn't do any good to
know a lot about arms control if nobody listened."

A few weeks earlier, at Christmas, Carolyn and I were invited
to the White House for a small dinner party. The subject of
trading arms with Iran was carefully avoided, but I eagerly
brought up another, more promising subject. "I don't want to
talk business with you, Mr. President," I said, "but in a few
days you're going to give the Citizenship Medal to the *Voyager*
crew, out in California." (Pilots Dick Rutan and Jeana Yeager
had circled the globe without refueling, sharing for one week a
cockpit the size of a phone booth.)

"Why don't you give them the Medal of Freedom?" I went
on. "These people epitomize all that you believe in: private en-
terprise, daring, a new world record without a dime of federal
support. Five years out there in a little town in the Mojave Desert, sleeping on the floor, putting it together. It's a feat up there
with Lindbergh crossing the Atlantic and Chuck Yeager breaking the sound barrier. It's the American dream."

The president, seated in the chair next to mine, cocked his
head and said, "Mike, I've got competent people at the White
House who make those decisions."

It seemed as if the twenty years I had worked for him had
vanished in the blink of an eye.

The answer puzzled me more than anything. But he was just
being Ronald Reagan, showing his loyalty to aides.

At the hospital, I told Bud McFarlane that, realistically, one
man can't shoulder all the blame. No one should carry that kind
of guilt or burden. When I left his room, I thought some more

about what I had said. I decided I was right, of course.

Driving home from Bethesda, I knew there was hope yet for all of us, for Reagan, and McFarlane, and Deaver, and the country. Or there would be enough blame to go around.

And whatever the next turn in my own fortunes, at least I would face it sober.

Epilogue:
The
Witness

Washington, D.C.

The start of my trial for perjury was postponed in mid-July 1987, just as Oliver North was completing his testimony in the Iran-Contra hearings. There was no connection, legal or spiritual, but I almost laughed out loud as I compared myself to the dashing marine colonel.

Here was Ollie North, boyish, handsome, macho, a combat veteran with a chestful of ribbons, with passion in his voice and a glint in his eye. What you would get if you mixed Huck Finn and Clint Eastwood.

Me? Balding, with horn-rimmed glasses and a temporary limp from a tennis knee. Nothing in common. I have been accused of lying and don't believe I did. North not only admitted that he lied and destroyed evidence, he bragged about it.

North emerged from the hearings with the kind of status usually associated with rock stars. Whether this was appropriate for a military officer and White House aide, the country was still trying to decide after the initial media furor settled down. No question, North put on a dazzling television show. He had an interesting capacity for turning teary-eyed when he talked about a few special subjects, such as himself.

I knew Oliver North pretty well, or thought I did. In my mind, the early description of him as a "loose cannon" came close to the mark. There was a tendency to believe he had vanquished that reputation with his performance on the witness stand. But I remembered North as one who loved the cloak-and-dagger stuff, so very full of himself, the type who goes around creating bad situations so he can make the best of them.

He came across to me as someone who was dangerous. I didn't know what he was doing—I suppose that sounds familiar—but I feared him. He was just too sure of his footing, too sure of his facts. He would fly to Beirut, be gone three days, and return as an expert.

For two reasons, I am tempted to place my judgment of Colonel North on hold. One, I recognize that I leave myself wide open in the glass-house category. Two, it isn't always wise to bet against someone who believes, as North does, against all odds, that he and the Contras will win out.

Still, I can't erase the feeling that Oliver North is the person at the center of the president's worst hour. I resent the fact that he seems not to understand that the policies he recklessly pursued embarrassed Ronald Reagan, divided and weakened the country.

It might have been even worse. In a curious way, I think the media missed the story. Their preoccupation was with the diversion of funds from the Iranian arms sale to the Nicaraguan Contras. Thus, at the outset, when it mattered most, attention was deflected from the ghastly reality that the United States had sold weapons to the Ayatollah Khomeini, whose Iranian fanatics had sponsored most of the world's recent terrorism, had taken Americans hostage and threatened American lives.

In 1981, I had watched from a few feet away the agony of Jimmy Carter, and saw Ronald Reagan take office with the vow that the United States would never be humiliated in such a way again.

From a distance, mired in my own troubles, I watched the president suffer as the Iran-Contra story unraveled. In the early stages, I think he was wounded less by the failure of the scheme than by the polls that showed a majority of Americans thought he was lying about what he did or did not know.

More than that, the people felt he was acting out of character. How could he fire North and call him a national hero? A marine colonel and a navy admiral took the Fifth Amendment and seemed to be protecting themselves instead of telling everything they knew to the president. At that point, my sense was that his supporters wanted him to do what Harry Truman did to Douglas MacArthur, with no regrets, if these were the two who had injured him.

Of course, a quick history lesson might be in order here. When Truman fired the general for exceeding his authority in Korea, MacArthur returned to a ticker-tape parade in New York and a national outpouring of admiration. Ronald Reagan's patience with North and Poindexter may not have been misguided, after all.

Poindexter impressed me as loyal and well balanced, a career military man who was limited by his political inexperience. I have no doubt that he did what he thought his president wanted—nor do I doubt that he misinterpreted what Reagan wanted. Unlike North, Poindexter was not someone who relished power or saw covert action as a sport.

Well after the hearings had ended, it was still hard to assemble a box score. Don Regan was out as chief of staff, Poindexter had accepted the blame for approving the diversion of funds, and the president had said the "ultimate" responsibility was his, while criticizing those who had kept him uninformed.

When the scandal first broke, I heard through the White House grapevine that a state of near-panic existed. North had shredded a small mountain of paper—one figure tossed around was up to ten thousand documents, letters, and memoranda. When it was learned that Bill Casey was dying of a brain tumor, some staffers—no, I won't name them—could scarcely contain their relief. As director of the Central Intelligence Agency, Casey was a logical candidate to be identified as the master planner. The secrets would be buried with him, and that would protect the president.

I didn't see it that way. Knowing Casey, I believed he was involved in the arms-to-Iran, cash-to-the Contras maneuvering. But to me his illness, and shortly his death, meant that questions would persist about what was discussed when Casey and Reagan met alone, as they often did. Rather than ending the speculation, Casey's death would almost assure that it continued.

Time would tell if the country accepted Poindexter as the architect of a plan that went awry. And the people had added a new phrase to their political vocabulary: "plausible deniability."

In fact, I felt that Casey would have tried to keep the details of the operation from the president, believing it to be in his best interest to do so. The scandal might never have happened, I believe, if Don Regan had not worked so hard at getting Nancy Reagan "out of the loop." Nancy was the one person who, getting wind of the affair, could have alerted the president to the facts—and the dangers.

But Regan wanted what he saw as Nancy's influence curtailed. And for longer than I would have predicted, she tolerated his brittle personality and high-handed ways. She would not have accepted from anyone else his famous remark, after the summit at Reykjavik, that his job was "to sweep up after the elephants."

Regan's days were numbered when Nancy went to the president and said flatly, "I can't deal with that man anymore." Reagan may have had private doubts before; from that point it was a matter of time.

The attempt by Don Regan to cling to his job was compared to the historic wartime scene when the army carried Sewell Avery, in his office chair, off the premises at Montgomery Ward, after he had refused to honor a court order.

Regan was at the president's elbow when the president said he would never stand in the way of someone who wanted to leave. That was as clear a signal as Ronald Reagan was ever going to give. Later, when reporters put the question to him, Regan replied: "Go ask *him*." I saw a lot of good people leave the White House, none with the lack of grace of Don Regan.

This combination, the Iran-Contra disclosures and Don Regan's long good-bye, led to some serious conclusion-jumping in the months ahead.

The president had met with Howard Baker in late February to

offer him the job as his chief of staff. While Baker rejoined his family in Florida to think it over, his closest aides, led by Jim Cannon, went to the White House to interview the senior staff.

After a day and a half of briefings, but without seeing the president, they delivered to Howard Baker a stunning report: If he accepted the post, he would have to be prepared at any time to invoke the 25th Amendment. The president, they had concluded, was on the brink of being physically and mentally incapable of carrying out his responsibilities.

Baker understood all the implications of that concern and they had to alarm him. He was never one to make a decision lightly. Now he returned to Washington, not knowing what to expect. He must have wondered if age had finally overtaken Ronald Reagan.

The next day, Baker and his top aides had a working lunch with the president and some of his Cabinet. Baker emerged from that meeting committed to the job, so much so that his enthusiastic statements puzzled much of the country. He said how impressed he was with the president's grasp of the issues, his alertness, his good health. The president was on top of things, he went on. The president was in charge.

To many listeners, Howard Baker seemed to be overreacting. His words sounded too defensive. But Baker was speaking as much to the White House team, and to a nervous Republican party, as he was to the public. He was telling them that he had not seen the feeble, distracted, unaware president others had described to him.

Baker's men concluded that they had been misled by the White House senior staff, who were mostly Don Regan sycophants.

Shortly thereafter, Jim Cannon sat in a meeting and heard someone refer to himself as "a Howard Baker man." Cannon quickly corrected him. "There are no Baker people here," he said, "only the president's people. And if anyone is uncomfortable with that, they ought to leave right now."

It had been a year and a half since that kind of talk had been heard around the White House.

It should come as no surprise that some of those who were in the most trusted positions would try to make themselves look good at the president's expense. The sad part is that they worked for a man who was above that sort of thing.

Reagan's health was called into question again with the publication of Bob Woodward's book on William Casey and the C.I.A. Casey was quoted as saying that the president's recovery from his gunshot wound was much slower, and less complete, than had been reported. A month or more after he left the hospital, Reagan was pictured as a near invalid. Alexander Haig jumped in to support that impression, saying that the White House staff had concealed the president's true condition from the country.

I do not deny that for twenty-four hours, perhaps even forty-eight, we were not certain of the president's survival. For a week, we may have worried about his effectiveness. But from that point on, his recovery was, if anything, ahead of schedule.

Of course, Al Haig's memory may be influenced by the need to still defend his "I'm-in-control" speech. Haig was there when the president held one of his first staff meetings after his return to the White House. So was I, along with Jim Baker, Ed Meese, and Dick Allen.

The president brought to the meeting a letter he had started in the hospital. Six pages long, handwritten on a yellow legal pad, the letter was addressed to Leonid Brezhnev. My guess was that he had been touched by the fact that he had come very close to death, and what he wrote to the Russian premier came from his heart. It may or may not take a large amount of stamina to write a six-page letter, but this one was not the work of a man crippled in flesh or spirit.

He began the letter by reminding Brezhnev that they had met once, at Richard Nixon's estate in California, Casa de Pacifica. He went on to say how much the world needed peace, and that the two of them really ought to think about the responsibility they had to future generations.

There were no proposals, just a direct and personal and thoughtful message to try to nudge the process along. Ronald Reagan was in his pajamas and bathrobe when he passed the letter around the room. "I don't know if you fellows will think it's a good idea," he said, "but why don't you read it and get back to me."

Dick Allen kept the letter, and a few days later, with the same group in place, he handed the president a somewhat shorter redraft of his letter, something the State Department might have written twenty years ago. Typical bureaucratese. We were each given a copy to read, and the president looked up from his and said, wearily, "Well, I guess you fellows know best. You're the experts."

I interrupted. "Mr. President, nobody elected anybody in the State Department or the National Security Council. Those guys have been screwing up for a quarter of a century. If you think that's a letter that ought to be sent to Brezhnev, don't let anyone change it. Why don't you just send it?"

He turned to Haig and said, "I agree with that. Send it the way I wrote it."

After everyone left, I was alone with Reagan in his study, and he thanked me for speaking up. "You know," he said, "I came to a conclusion about something when I was in the hospital. There must be a reason why I was spared. From now on, I'm going to follow my own instincts."

The letter was mailed—in its original form. A few weeks later, the president received a reply from Mr. Brezhnev. It was short and impersonal and, apparently, written by some bureaucrat in the Kremlin.

By now most of the players have left the stage. Brezhnev is dead. Haig in late 1987 was running for president. The always-loyal Ed Meese is still on the job, but the rest of us are pretty well scattered.

Quite unintentionally, the act of leaving has become one of the themes of this book. It will not come too soon for the Reagans, and that thought saddens me. There is much that is left unfinished: my trial, the Iran-Contra story, the final verdict on the Reagan presidency. But few tasks ever really get finished in politics.

You just turn another page.

Index